The History and Traditions of Mallerstang Forest and Pendragon Castle

William Nicholls

Kirkby Stephen Press
Kirkby Stephen, Cumbria

www. kirkbystephenpress. co.uk

@ New introduction and layout Kirkby Stephen Press, 2014

First published 1883, John Heywood, Manchester
This paperback edition 2014

ISBN : 978-0-9928045-0-3 Paperback

This publication reproduces the text of the original edition.
The content has not been altered or updated. Kirkby Stephen
Press has no responsibility for the accuracy of the information
contained in this publication and does not guarantee that the
content is, or will remain, accurate.

Typesetting by typesetter.org.uk
The front cover illustration is a reproduction from the original 1883 edition
Illustrations reproduced by Jane Tilley
Printed by Charlesworth Group, Wakefield, West Yorkshire

This important historical work was originally published in 1883 and is now in the "public domain".

The complete text has been reset to reproduce the original format as closely as possible and to maintain the integrity of the work as a whole. Minor errors in reproduction have been kept to a minimum to optimise content accessibility. The original title page is included overleaf and there is an added introduction for this edition.

Otherwise the original layout and size remain the same.

INTRODUCTION TO THE NEW EDITION

By the time this original volume was published *circa* 1883 Britain had experienced forty years in which the country had been transformed from a picturesque, chaotic world into a more orderly and democratic nation. An element of this new order is probably reflected in the motives for this work and one of its companions *The History and Traditions of Ravenstonedale* both authored by William Nicholls. The latter parish had been in the forefront of religious dissent in the preceding centuries firstly with the early Quakers of the seventeenth century and then under the lordly patronage of the later Whartons. By 1880 both Ravenstonedale and Mallerstang along with the rest of Westmorland would have experienced the impact of the railway being home to two Anglo-Scottish routes and various link and branch lines. Tebay was a major employer and Kirkby Stephen became host to two railway stations for the Settle-Carlisle and Stainmore lines. The railway transported produce and people but also improved the spread of news and ideas.

The Rev William Nicholls was the minister of High Chapel Congregational Church, Ravenstonedale (in the former county of Westmorland) from 1869 to 1883. He was born in Bristol in 1835 and had entered Lancashire College in 1855. He died in 1921 at the age of 86 and is buried at High Chapel along with his wife Marianne *(nee* Chamberlain) the daughter of a Congregational minister. A contemporary obituary said; *retiring in his disposition but greatly beloved.* High Chapel closed for worship in 2006 and is now used as a Community Centre by Ravenstonedale Parish Council. The Mallerstang history was Nicholls' second book preceded by a first volume for Ravenstonedale. A second Ravenstonedale volume appeared in about 1914. By the time the Mallerstang volume was published Nicholls had moved to Blackford Bridge, Bury and retired to Prestwich in 1899 where he wrote further histories of both Prestwich and Radcliffe.

Kirkby Stephen Press 2014

THE
HISTORY AND TRADITIONS
OF
MALLERSTANG FOREST
AND
PENDRAGON CASTLE

BY THE
REV. W. NICHOLLS

(AUTHOR OF "THE HISTORY AND TRADITIONS OF RAVENSTONEDALE")

MANCHESTER: JOHN HEYWOOD, DEANSGATE AND RIDGEFIELD.
LONDON: JOHN HEYWOOD; SIMPKIN, MARSHALL, & CO. KIRKBY STEPHEN: J.
W. BRAITHWAITE. APPLEBY: J. WHITEHEAD. PENRITH: J. HODGSON. KENDAL:
ATKINSON & POLLITT, AND E. GILL. SEDBERGH: JACKSON & SONS. SETTLE:
WILDMAN & SON. HAWES: J. HISCOCK.
[ALL RIGHTS RESERVED.)

THIS WORK IS
Respectfully Dedicated
BY PERMISSION

TO

LORD HOTHFIELD OF HOTHFIELD

LORD LIEUTENANT OF WESTMORLAND

AND

LORD OF THE MANOR OF MALLERSTANG

BY THE AUTHOR.

PREFACE.

HEREWITH I send forth another atom of English History. Encouraged by the reception given to the "History and Traditions of Ravenstonedale" by the people of this district, I have ventured to call their attention to an adjoining dale, different though no less interesting in the features of its history. A modern writer has said, "It has often been remarked that in England, if attention is called to some little, unknown and obscure hamlet, a little research into its records will reveal to the astonishment of the interested enquirer how, in the ages long ago deceased, it was the home of great historic characters and the centre of rich historic circumstances." These words may be applied to Mallerstang Forest and Pendragon Castle. When the reader bears in mind that the dale is not more than five miles in length, he will probably be surprised that so much material could have been gathered together respecting so small a dale. This, however, should be said, that it contains two or three objects of special interest; that a river the Eden – rises in it, and pursues its way through its bottom, receiving tributaries on its east and west. The Episcopal Chapel is of undoubtedly early date, and the Castle of Pendragon, now a ruin, would be enough of itself to invest the dale with uncommon interest. It has been my aim to obtain accurate as well as ample information, and to present it to the reader in a reliable and attractive form. I am under deep obligation to many contributors for different kinds of information. Perhaps the one to whom I owe the most, Mr. G. Blades, who conversed with me with great interest and animation on the social life of the inhabitants in his early days, did not live to hear the delivery of the first lecture. He was a good – almost a typical – specimen of the statesman. He farmed his own land. He had been born and brought up in his own dale, and knew every inch of it. He was conservative in his ideas. He did not care for railway trains, and never travelled in them; he regarded them as an innovation on the good old times. Take him all in all, he was an intelligent and reliable man, of whom the people of any dale might have been proud. I desire to recognise the kind help of Canon Simpson, who took the chair for me at the first lecture, and whose well deserved praise as an archaeologist is in all the county. Captain Grimshaw also sent me some valuable material, and Edward Heelis, Esq., and to the Rev. W. Thompson, of Sedbergh, and the Rev. T. Wharton, of Stainmore, and not omitting Miss Fawcett, of The Thrang, I am indebted for notes and literary assistance. There are others that I might name, but I must not omit Mr. J. Dickenson, whose precise and clear recollections of the past I have found invaluable.

The lectures were delivered in the Board School Room, Mallerstang, kindly lent by the School Board on each occasion.

W. N.

Manchester Road, Bury.
March 28, 1883.

CONTENTS.

	Page
Lecture I	9
Lecture II	23
Lecture III	47
Lecture IV	93
Appendix	122
List of Subscribers	127

LECTURE I.

THERE are few dales in Westmorland more isolated and sequestered than that of Mallerstang. In no part of it is the bottom of the valley more than half a mile in breadth, and in some parts not that, with a ridge of hills rising, one on either side, and almost perpendicularly to a height of over two thousand feet. This accounts for the phenomenon which you have noticed in your dale, that the wind always blows up or down the valley. From the motion of the clouds you see that it may blow from the east or the west, but to you it is north or south. The formation of the grand walls of the dale, geologists tell us, is mostly carboniferous limestone and shale, and that the valley was scooped out by the action of running water, which has eaten down deep into the solid crust, leaving the two ridges of Wild Boar Fell on the one hand, and Hugh's Seat on the other. Could we, however, transport ourselves into the dim and far – reaching past, we should see those two ridge summits connected by a table-land instead of what we now see – a picturesque and romantic valley. And I confess, at the outset, that I was drawn into an enquiry into the history and traditions of your dale, not on account of its social, commercial, or political importance, but mostly owing to the fascination which its scenery has exercised upon my mind, together with its most remarkable memorial – the ruin of Pendragon Castle – which Whellan, in his "History of Westmorland," says, is "one of the most interesting relics of antiquity in the county."

The name of the dale is, as you know, Mallerstang Forest, and it is a township of the parish of Kirkby Stephen. The etymology of the name I have been unable to find a trace of; and, instead of guessing what it might be, perhaps it would be better to leave it as one of the things of the past which we cannot know.*

In all the old writings it is called Mallerstang Forest. Now in such documents we find, notably in Blackstone, that the word forest did not mean what we understand it to mean today, a considerable extent of land thickly covered with trees, but a piece of waste ground given up to game – in fact, a chase. Whellan, in his history of this county, says, "This district was anciently a vast forest, inhabited by every description of game." And that this was the character of the Mallerstang Forest we have evidence. For example; it is on record in the "Appleby Sessions Indictment Book," "That at a petty sessions, held Michaelmas, 1665, before Sir Philip Musgrave, Knight and Bart., Sir John Lowther, Bart., Sir John Lowther the younger, Bart., and John Dalston, Esquire, four of His Majesty's justices of the peace, Thomas Knewstubb, Ralph Shaw, Henry Shaw, Thomas Whitfield, Adam Fothergill, Robert Guy, Richard Heseltine, and Henry Dixon were convicted of

---

* Since writing the above, I have met with the following etymology of the name in Whitaker's "History and Antiquities of the Deanery of Craven." He says: "This wild tract was, I suppose, so called Mallard Stank, the pool of the Mallard, referring to some early expansion of the Eden which has long since burst its mounds." The Rev. J. Wharton, of Stainmore, has also sent me the following note to the like effect: "Mallerstang (Mallard Stagnum), morass of the wild duck; compare Dun-Mallard (Ullswater) and Garstang."

killing a deer within the Forest of Mallerstange, belonging to the honourable Ann, Countess Dowager of Dorset, Pembroke, and Montgomerye, who, on examination, confessed, and were each of them fined £20, according to the statute."* And tradition says that the last deerkeeper in Mallerstang lived in a place called Ridding House, from near which he could see a large portion of the forest, and when he saw anyone disturbing the deer he used to shout at them with such stentorian lungs, that he could be heard a long distance, and went by the name of "Gobe."

Still it is evident that, at a period anterior to the seventeenth century, of which I have been speaking, this dale was well wooded, and the trees that grew here were mostly birch and alder, and hazel bushes, and some oak, but not much. As we might expect, the land is rich in fuel for fire, from turf down to black hard peat, and this, until about thirty years ago, previous to the introduction of railways, supplied most of the inhabitants with fuel; and so well did the folks keep themselves supplied with peat, that if they had a wet season, a great many of them had enough for the following year.

The first name connected with the dale of which we possess any record is Uther Pendragon. He is a half historical and half-mythical person; he is, so to speak, in the dim twylight between legend and history. It is not my business here to enter upon the value of oral tradition handed down through the ages from sire to son; but of this we are sure, that the recollections of the people and the evidence of the oldest extant documents show that the castle in your midst was always called Pendragon Castle. Now in Geoffrey of Monmouth's British History I find a record of Uther

---

*For the above extract I have pleasure in acknowledging the kindness of Canon Machell, who has the Hill's' Westmorland MSS. in his possession, and from which, at the request of Miss A. N. Hill, he copied it. Vol. iii., page 405.

Pendragon. I am aware that he is not a high authority; still he lived in the early part of the twelfth century; and I give you his account of Uther Pendragon, which, after the spirit of the age, is no doubt mixed up with legend. He says:

"During these transactions at Winchester [the murder of Aurelius Ambrosius, the brother of Uther, by poisoning] there appeared a star of wonderful magnitude and brightness, darting forth a ray at the end of which was a globe of fire in the form of a dragon, out of whose mouth issued forth two rays; one of which seemed to stretch out itself beyond the extent of Gaul, the other towards the Irish Sea, and ended in seven lesser rays. At the appearance of this star a general fear and amazement seized the people; and even Uther, the king's brother, who was then upon his march with his army into Cambria, being not a little terrified at it was very curious to know of the learned men what it portended.

"Among others, he ordered Merlin [Merlin was a sage who was supposed to possess a measure of prophetic insight] to be called, who also attended in this expedition to give his advice in the management of the war; and who being now presented before him, was commanded to discover to him the signification of the star. At this he burst out into tears, and with a loud voice cried out: 'O, irreparable loss! O, distressed people of Britain! Alas, the illustrious prince is departed! The renowned king of the Britons, Aurelius Ambrosius, is dead! whose death will prove fatal to us all unless God be our helper. Make haste, therefore, most noble Uther, make haste to engage the enemy; the victory shall be yours, and you shall be king of all Britain. For the star and the fiery dragon under it signifies yourself, and the ray extending towards the Gallic coast portends that you shall have a most potent son, to whose power all those kingdoms shall be subject over which the ray reaches. But the other ray signifies a daughter, whose sons and grandsons shall successively enjoy the kingdom of Britain.'" The chronicler, after having referred to the death of Aurelius Ambrosius, which had actually taken place, proceeds: "Uther, the brother of the deceased king, having assembled the clergy of the kingdom, took the crown, and by universal consent was advanced to the kingdom. And remembering the explanation which Merlin had made of the star above mentioned, he commanded two dragons to be made of gold in likeness of the dragon which he had seen at the ray of the star. As soon as they were done with wonderful nicety of workmanship, he made a present of one to the Cathedral of Winchester [there are many legends of various kinds of King Arthur, his son, connected with this cathedral still]; but reserved the other for himself, to be carried along with him to the wars. From this time, therefore, he was called Uther Pendragon, which in the British tongue signifies the dragon's head; the occasion of this appellation being Merlin's predicting from the appearance of a dragon that he should be a king."

The preceding has a mythical cast, and any historian would accept it with caution; still the substratum of it may be true. In the year of our Lord 420, after the Romans had left the island, we know that the Britons, no longer overawed by the presence of the Roman legions, refused to acknowledge the authority of the provincial and municipal governors of Rome, and restored the power of the ancient chiefs under the supremacy of an elective monarch, who bore the title of Pendragon, and administered the affairs of the central government. The word *pen* is British for head, and *dragon* for leader or chief. Dr. Milner Fothergill, in writing to me on this subject, says: "Pendragon was the generalissimo of the united Cymric tribes. Uter was in all probability the Pendragon of the Cumbrian Cymri who long held their own against the tide of Saxons." And I am disposed to accept this view of the chief from whom the castle here takes its name. For is there anything fabulous or even improbable in the fact that such a monarch would build a stronghold in this valley, which is the best outlet from the north into the Craven district and the midlands of England? And if he did, would it not be likely to be remembered? Moreover, Whitaker, after speaking of Pendragon Castle, proceeds: "With respect to the name, which, among authentic records, *first appears* in an inquisition of the 8th Edward II. [1314-5], I shall only observe that, as this place was certainly included in the limits of the Strath Cluyd Britons, a fortress might really have been erected on the spot by Uther. It is easy to defer too little as well as too much to remote tradition." It is not probable that Uther Pendragon often lived here, or that the original castle was intended to be other than a keep in a most important military position.

Nicholson and Burn, in their "History of Westmorland," give quite another and a different account of Uther Pendragon, and here is what they say:

"The Castle of Mallerstang, called Pendragon Castle, is said to have been built about the time of Vortigern by Uter Pendragon."

So far this agrees with Geoffrey of Monmouth. The writer proceeds, "Who this Uter was may be difficult to ascertain. There was a family of the name of Ughtred of ancient time; and during the time of the Saxons in England before the Norman conquest there was a famous warrior of the name of Uchtred, son of Waltheof, Earl of Northumberland, who, with a much inferior army, gave the Scots under their king Malcolm a most signal overthrow, for which victory King Ethelred gave to Uchtred his daughter, the Princess Elgiva, in marriage, and with her the counties of Northumberland and York for a portion. Pendragon seems not to be properly the name of a man, but an epithet only, describing his warlike quality. Pen, it is well known, signifies a mountain or something that is great, and dragon hath been applied in all ages to military persons."

The radical defect of Dr. Burns' account of Uter Pendragon is, that the link is wanting that should connect Uchtred, the Saxon warrior, with the castle here. He received with his wife, we are told, Northumberland and York for a portion. Pendragon Castle is in neither of those counties, and the name of its founder was Uther and not Uchtred. Moreover, there is a tradition current in the district that the Saxons besieged the castle, and, considering it impregnable, resorted to treachery, and poisoned the well – which is still pointed out to visitors -and that Uther and his garrison were poisoned, owing to drinking of its water. This is as much as I have been able to glean of Uther Pendragon. All are agreed, however, that he lived in ancient British or early Saxon times; and as an evidence of how thoroughly his existence has entered into the traditions of the people, I have it, on the authority of Canon Simpson, that to this day the ghost of Old Uther is said to appear on Shap Fell. He was the first chief of this dale. Few were the inhabitants here; indeed we have evidence that the only inhabitants were those who lived in the castle. Solemn must have been the scene; the castle, rude and massive, set in a forest of trees, the hiding-place of the wild boar and the wolf.

The first lord of the manor, properly so called, of whom we have any record, is Hugh de Moreville, a much less undefined person than Uther Pendragon. The highest point of the eastern ridge is called Hugh's Seat, where Anne, Countess of Pembroke, erected a stone pillar, and upon it the inscription is cut, A.P. 1664. There is a tradition current amongst the people that upon this mountain he concealed himself during a Scotch invasion. Another that I have met with is that after he had been hunting he sat down there and partook of refreshment. This is incontrovertible, that he was one of the four knights who murdered the Archbishop Thomas a Becket, in Canterbury Cathedral, in the year 1170. The other knights engaged in the bloody deed were Reginald Fitzurse, Richard Brito, and William de Tracy, but with them at present we are not concerned, except that this should be said in extenuation of all, that they received their first hint from the king, Henry II., when he was holding his court at Bur, near Bayeux, at which they were present. Now a hint from the king, which could not be easily misunderstood, amounted to a command to loyal knights. They crossed the Channel, proceeded to Canterbury, secured an interview with a Becket, which they did not wish to be of a pacific character, and after mutual recrimination in the palace, on which I need not enter, the archbishop fled for refuge into the cathedral, whither he was followed by his assailants, and there, in the deepening twilight of December 29th, 1170, he was murdered. I am indebted to Dean Stanley's "Historical Memorials of Canterbury" for the following facts; and every allusion to De Moreville is, to his credit, that whatever blame may be awarded to the perpetrators of this crime, the lightest share must rest upon him. Dean Stanley, after referring to the other knights, says, "Moreville was of higher rank and office than the others. He was this very year Justice Itinerant of the counties of Northumberland and Cumberland, where he inherited the barony of Burgh-on-the-Sands, and other possessions, from his father Roger and his grandfather Simon. He was, likewise, forester of Cumberland, owner of the Castle of Knaresborongh, and added to his paternal property that of his wife, Helwise de Stute-ville." The following is the next allusion: "He, the archbishop, in his turn complained of the insults he had received. First came the grand grievances of the preceding week. 'They have attacked my servants, they have cut off my sumpter mule's tail, they have carried off the casks of wine that were the king's own gift.' It was now that Hugh de Moreville, the gentlest of the four, put in a milder answer: 'Why did you not complain to the king of these outrages? Why do you take upon yourself to punish them by your own authority?' The archbishop turned round sharply upon him. 'Hugh, how proudly yon lift up your head! When the rights of the Church are violated I shall wait for no man's permission to avenge them. I will give to the king the things that are the king's, but to God the things that are God's. It is my business, and I alone will see to it.'" The historian adds: "For the first time in the interview the archbishop had assumed an attitude of defiance."

Later on in the account we read: "Hugh of Horsea planted his foot on the neck of the corpse, thrust his sword into the ghastly wound, and scattered his brains over the pavement. 'Let us go; let us go,' he said, in conclusion, 'the traitor is dead; he will rise no more.' This was the final act. One only of the four knights had struck no blow. Hugh de Moreville throughout retained the gentler disposition for which he was distinguished, and contented himself with holding back at the entrance of the transept the crowds who were pouring in through the nave."

After the murder the four knights hastened to Saltwood, where they stayed for the night; and tradition states that they proceeded together to the residence of Hugh de Moreville at Knaresborough, where they remained for twelve months. During this year he was discontinued from his office of Justice Itinerant in the counties of Northumberland and Cumberland.

This was done to appease popular indignation, rather than as a punishment inflicted by the king; for within the first two years of the murder the murderers were living at Court in Normandy on familiar terms with the king, and constantly joined him in the pleasures of the chase, or else hawking and hunting in England. And in the first year of King John, Hugh de Moreville is recorded as paying twenty five marks, and three palfreys for holding his Court as Justice Itinerant in the counties of Northumberland and Cumberland, so long as Helwise, his wife, shall continue in a secular habit. He procured about the same period a charter for a fair and market at Kirkoswald, and died shortly afterwards, leaving two daughters. There is a legend that he and the other knights went on a pilgrimage of expiation to the Holy Land, and died there; but it is a myth that arose out of the superstitions that, like a nimbus, gathered around the name and memory of *Saint* Thomas a Becket. Hugh de Moreville visited the north after having been a spectator of the tragedy, for in all the representations of the martyrdom, in painted windows or in ancient frescoes, Hugh de Moreville is stationed aloof from the massacre. On his way from Knaresborough he must have passed through this dale, and, no doubt, rested for awhile in Pendragon Castle. In strange contrast were the grand and sombre surroundings of this Westmorland dale to the scenes of excitement which he had previously witnessed. Would that some Boswell had been with him in the stronghold, and given to us a few of his spoken thoughts. However, your mountain bearing the name of Hugh's Seat will ever associate you with one, despite the crime, of noble spirit and bearing.

We learn that the sister of Hugh de Moreville, named Maud, married Wm. de Veteripont, with whom he received the manor and estate of the county. But Henry II., to appease the indignation of his subjects occasioned by the murder of the Archbishop, not only suspended him temporarily from the office of Justice Itinerant of the counties of Northumberland and Cumberland, but confiscated the property, and granted the castle of Appleby to the custody of Gospatric, son of Orme, but the barony was retained by the crown till King John restored it to the family by granting it to Robert de Veteripont. He died in 1228, and was succeeded by John de Veteripont, who died about the year 1242, leaving his infant son, Robert de Veteripont, a ward to the king, and in the guardianship of the Prior of Carlisle. Now we learn that during the minority of Robert de Veteripont the Prior of Carlisle permitted great waste to be committed, and particularly on an inquisition thereof being taken, it was found that the Vale of Mallerstang was much decayed by the multitude of vaccaries. Vaccaries mean large enclosed cow pastures. During the period of the minority of Robert de Veteripont it is evident that different persons had made vaccaries in the forest, and had probably erected houses in them of a very simple and primitive kind. It would appear that game also had been to some extent destroyed by one Roger, the forester, and other archers from Lundsdale. From one point of view the breaking in upon the forest was a deterioration of it; but from another, and a higher, it was one of the steps of advancement in this district towards civilisation.

The name of the lord of the manor changes again. One of the daughters of Robert de Veteripont married Roger de Clifford, of Clifford Castle on the Wye in Herefordshire, who becomes lord of the manor, and we are told that after the death of Roger de Clifford in 11th of Edward I. [1283] it was found by inquisition that the forest of Mallorstang in herbage and agistment, and all other issues, was worth yearly £44 7s. 6d.

From the authority of Mr. Geo. Blades, an aged man in the dale (now deceased), I learn that the same sum is paid to the lord of the manor to-day, and that it has never varied much. Two pieces of land have been sold by the lord of the manor, and these are not subject to the lord's rent; they are Shor Gill and Moor Riggs. To make up for this deficiency of lord's rent, encroachments have been made upon the common, and these have been charged lord's rent. The value of money we know has diminished greatly, still the loss has been borne by the lord of the manor.

And now passing over many of the successive lords of the manor who did not specially identify themselves with this dale – and it is mainly in this connection it is our business to regard them – I come to Anne, Countess of Pembroke. George Clifford, the Earl of Cumberland, was born in Brougham Castle, August 8th, 1558. He signalised himself in the service of Queen Elizabeth, and was a person of great activity of body, sprightliness of wit, and civility of demeanour. He was one of the commissioners who tried and condemned the unfortunate Mary Queen of Scots, and one of the four earls present at her execution. He died, leaving an only daughter, Anne, born in Skipton Castle, January 30th, 1591. She married first, Richard Sackville, Lord Buckhurst, afterwards Earl of Dorset, by whom she had issue Margaret and Isabella; the latter of whom was married to James Compton, Earl of Northampton, by whom she had six children, who all died without issue, so that Margaret became the sole heiress of the Clifford family. Her second husband was Philip Herbert, Earl of Pembroke and Montgomery, whom she survived from 1649 to 1675, when she died, having spent her long widowhood in the north of England in repairing her castles and in works of public and private charity. Weekly distribution and daily alms were given at her gate. The consumption of her household she regularly purchased with ready money in the towns and villages around her, seldom procuring anything from London, being desirous the county might benefit by her. Many of her diaries in which she regularly entered the occurrences of the day down to the minutest details, and the names of all strangers that came to the house, whether on busines or otherwise, are very amusing. Evidently she was a lady of strong character, and her mind was rather of the masculine than the feminine type. In treating of the castle and the chapel I shall have to refer to this lady again.

After the death of the Countess of Pembroke her elder daughter, Margaret, became sole heir of the Clifford family. She was espoused in 1629 by John Lord Tufton, afterwards Earl of Thanet, a title that had been conferred upon his father by Charles I., in 1628. The estates and title next devolved upon his brother Rupard, who died unmarried in 1683, when he was succeeded by Thomas, the fourth brother, who established his claim to the title and barony of Lord Clifford, first granted to his maternal ancestor, Richard de Clifford, in A.D. 1300. He died in 1729, when he was succeeded by his nephew, Sackville Tufton, who was succeeded by his son of the same name, who died in Italy, March, 1786, when his son, Sackville Tufton, the ninth earl, succeeded; and he, dying without issue in 1825, was succeeded by his brother, Charles Tufton, the tenth earl, who died unmarried in April, 1832, when the title and estates descended to his brother, Henry Tufton, the eleventh earl, who died unmarried, 12th June, 1849. After his death the title became extinct, and all his estates passed to Sir Richard Tufton, naturalised 1849, created a baronet, 1851, and died 20th June, 1871. He was succeeded by his son, Sir Henry J. Tufton, who was appointed Lord Lieutenant of Westmorland in 1881, and in the same year elevated to the peerage as Baron Hothfield of Hothfield, by the present Government. We wish the present lord of the manor long life and great enjoyment of the honour which has been deservedly put upon him. In 1880, during the contested election, we learnt that on this side of the county he was regarded with enthusiasm. He was born on the 4th of June, 1844, and is now (1882) consequently in his thirty-ninth year.

LECTURE II.

> The British bards that tuned their lyres
> To Arthur and Pendragon's praise. – *Sir Walter Scott.*

I SHALL now call your attention to Pendragon Castle. Every student of history knows that the castle occupied a very considerable place in the life of the people in the early and middle ages. Some of them, like your own, were not baronial residences, so much as strongholds; it was almost impossible for them to be taken: a few men barred and bolted within could defy whole armies without.

They were usually built on an eminence, or on the bank of a river which could be made to serve wholly or partially the purpose of a moat as in the case of your own castle which is built on the eastern bank of the Eden. If it be true to its name it was built originally by Uther Pendragon; and has been for ages a grim grand keep. Would that we could tell from precise historical data how long. Canon Simpson, who is an authority in such matters, says, in notes which he contributed to a local magazine, "There was doubtless a castle or stronghold here *long before* the Conquest which its then owner, Uther, endeavoured to strengthen by drawing around it the waters of the Eden."

The form of the original castle was very different from that of the present ruin of the last restoration which took place, as we shall see further on, in the year 1660 upon much older foundations. Probably the pre-Norman castle was a round tower, though this can of course be but conjecture. Whitaker, in his "History of Craven," gives it as his opinion "that the castles of Brugh, Appleby, Pendragon, and Brougham were built by Ranulph de Meschines, the knight to whom William the Conqueror gave this part of the country. Brough to fortify the pass of Stainmore; Pendragon that of Mallerstang; Appleby, for its central as well as strong and beautiful situation in the barony; and Brougham to guard its northern boundary." "Pendragon Castle," he further observes, "equally romantic in name and situation, though manifestly of the same age, is of a different form from all the rest. It has been one of those low square Norman castles, which having had no bailey [for the benefit of the unlearned in such terms I observe that a bailey is the space immediately within a surrounding wall and the castle] enclosed a small area, and had many diminutive apartments opening inward." Canon Sirnpson is of opinion that these apartments or recesses were probably used as sleeping rooms, a curtain or screen being drawn before them, and thus separating them from the more public apartment. The day will come, perhaps, when the stones and rubbish which at present fill up the enclosure will be removed, and the clearance will, in my opinion, reveal some interesting facts with respect to the building.*

---

* Robert Rennison, our well-known Ravenstonedale postman, told me a few weeks ago, that when he was a boy, whilst he and Robert Hutchinson were climbing amongst the ruins of the castle one moonlight night in search of young owls, and they obtained two, they picked up three copper coins; he does not remember what they were, nor their date; probably they were modern.

We learn from inquisitions that were taken that Robert de Veteripont became ward of the Prior of Carlisle in the 26th year of Henry III. [1241], and that he so far neglected his duties as to permit great waste to be committed on his estates; and particularly that of the Vale of Mallerstang, was much decayed by the multitude of vaccaries, *i.e.,* cow pastures, and chiefly by the archery of "Roger the forester." The name of this man still lingers amongst the people as an individual of strong and defiant character. Probably if we were living nearer to the period, there would be current anecdotes told concerning him, just as there still are in the neighbourhood of Sherwood Forest of "bold Robin Hood."

There were also, we are informed by the same authority, other archers of Lundsdale; also purprestures, *i.e.,* encroachments, were made in many places within the forest and in the boundary of the forest, by sufferance of the said Prior after he took upon him the guardianship.

"In the 8th Edward II. [1314] the jurors find that in the Vale of Mallerstang there is one castle called Pendragon, with a vaccary held by Andrew de Harcla of the rent of 6d. a year." In that year – 1314 – Robert de Clifford, the owner of Pendragon, died fighting for the king at Bannockburn. His eldest son was at that time about 15 years old. The strong probability, therefore, is, that Andrew de Harcla was invited by the Clifford family to take charge of Pendragon Castle during his minority, at a rent that was merely nominal.

Roger de Clifford came of age in 1321, but fought against the king in his adherence to the Earl of Lancaster at Borough Bridge, 1322, when he was taken prisoner, and his lands forfeited to the king. He died in 1327.

Then again in the lst Edward III. [1327] the jurors find that belonging to Roger de Clifford, deceased, was the castle of

Pendragon, together with the forest of Mallerstang to the same belonging; that the buildings of the castle cannot be extended, for that the costs of maintaining the same exceed the profits thereof. Also that in the said forest there are divers vaccaries, and other profits of herbage in the hands of tenants at will, who pay yearly – at Martinmas and Whitsuntide, £30.

Anne, Countess of Pembroke, relates in her memoirs that "Idonea de Veteripont, one of the daughters and co-heiresses of Robert de Veteripont, who married Roger de Leyburn, made a great part of her residence in Westmorland at Brugh Castle, under Stanemore, and at Pendragon Castle in Mallerstang, and the latter place -i.e., Pendragon Castle was her chief and beloved habitation." From this we may conclude that she loved retirement, and to be under the influence of your grand hills. She died here in Pendragon Castle in 1334. Also at this castle, we learn from Whitaker, in 1337 Edward Baliol was honourably received, on his expulsion out of Scotland, by Robert de Clifford, and entertained with magnificent hunting in the adjoining forest of Mallerstang. The lord of the manor in this way most fully shewed the honours of hospitality to one who makes himself momentarily conspicuous in history by his daring and successful invasion of Scotland, then under the Regency of Randolph, Earl of Morey, in 1332. Accompanied by some English noblemen bent on recovering their forfeited estates in Scotland, he landed with a few hundred followers at Kinghorn, in Fifeshire, defeated the Earl of Fife, pushed boldly into the country, and in Dupplin moor, in Perthshire, routed with immense slaughter an army upwards of ten times more numerous than his own. On the 24th September, seven weeks from the date of his landing, he was crowned King of Scotland at Scone. He had only enjoyed the kingly dignity for about three months when he was surprised in his camp at Annan, and nearly lost his life, as well as the crown he had so recently assumed. Subsequently he was expelled from Scotland. We are not told how long he remained an honoured visitor in Pendragon Castle, enjoying the hospitality of Robert de Clifford, but during the visit the forest was gay by day with magnificent hunting, and the castle brilliant by night.

In 1341 the castle was burnt down by the Scots. This was in the 15th year of Edward III., during a period of fierce hostility between the two kingdoms, which ended in the defeat of the Scottish army at Nevil's Cross, near Durham, and the taking of the Scottish king, David II., prisoner. The castle was restored, however, and in the year 1541 was again reduced to ruin. The cause of its ruin on this occasion I cannot ascertain; it took place in the 32nd year of the reign of Henry VIII. Henry, son of Henry Lord Clifford, and Ann St. John, his wife, was lord of the manor. He was afterwards created Earl of Cumberland, by Henry VIII., and Knight of the Garter. He was several times Lord Warden of the Marches, and behaved with great nobleness and gallantry in the wars against Scotland; and possibly the castle was on this occasion also demolished by the Scots; To this ruin Camden refers in his history. And when you remember that the materials for his history came no lower than 1589, you will see clearly that he became conversant with the ruin in the lifetime of those who must have remembered the demolition. He says: "The noble river Eden, called by Ptolemy, Ituna, rising in Yorkshire (?), has at first only a small stream; but increasing gradually by the confluence of several little rivers seeks a passage through these mountains to the north-west, by Pendragon Castle, to which age has left nothing but the name and a great heap of stones." In a note to the above, Edward Gibson, who translated and edited the work in 1695, says: "Pendragon Castle was not a great heap of stones in Mr.

Camden's time; when the walls, being four yards in thickness (with battlements upon them), were standing till the year 1660, that the most noble lady, the Lady Anne Clifford, Conntess Dowagcr of Pembroke, Dorset, and Montgomery, repaired this ancient home of her ancestors, with three more castles which she had in this county, and removing frequently from one to another, kept hospitality and diffused her charity all over the country. This castle is washed on the east by the river Eden; and on the other sides there are great trenches, as if the first builder had intended to draw the water round it. But the attempt proved ineffectual, from whence they have an old rhyme hereabouts—

> Let Uter Pen dragon do what he can,
> The river Eden will run where it ran."

There are two or three statements in this extract which need remark, and the first is, that Gibson is somewhat severe on his author in saying that it was not a heap of stones possibly it was not in the most literal sense; for in the inscription that appeared over the castle gate we learn that
"it had layen ruinous without timber or any covering ever since the year 1541." From this it would appear clearly that the castle was uninhabitable, which is probably what Camden meant by the expression "a heap of stones." Gibson also says that the castle is washed on the east by the river Eden; it is on the west. The well known couplet as at present rendered by the people is:

> "Let Uter Pendmgon do what he can
> Eden will run w here Eden ran."

This saying is frequently appropriated and applied to express determination and firmness. Carefully I have enquired into its history, and have discovered merely, that it is very ancient. The objection to the possibility of the attempt that occurs to the visitor is, that the bed of the river is at present very much below the castle. It is possible however, that it has worn down its bed during the last 1,000 or 1,300 years. Undoubtedly the moat is only partly made. Dr. Simpson says – "Uter endeavoured to strengthen the stronghold by drawing around it the waters of the Eden. The stream which is sometimes much swollen and rapid was however, too much for him, the dam which he had made across the river was washed down, and the memory of this attempt to turn the water out of its usual course, only remains in the old proverb." Anne, Countess of Pembroke, restored the castle in 1660 A.D., and in her diary she says she formed the design of restoring it so early as the year 1615 for a library for Mr. C. Wolridge. On its restoration, the following inscription cut upon a stone was over the entrance gate – "This Pendragon Castle was repayred by the Lady Ann Clifford, Countess dowager of Pembroke, Dorset, and Montgomerie, and Vescie, High Sheriffesse, by inheritance, of the county of Westmorland, and Lady of the honour of Skipton in Craven, in the year 1660 so as she came to lye in it herself for a little while in October, 1661; after it had layen ruinous without timber or any covering ever since the year 1541. Isaiah Chap. 58, ver. 12. God's name be praised."

She also built a bridge here over the Eden; and in 1662 we learn from her memoirs "a wall of lime and stone round the piece of ground she had caused to be taken in being quarters high, and ninety roods in compass, with two gates, and within it a stable, coach house, brew house, bake house, wash house, and a little chamber over the gate that is arched." The buildings here referred to were outside the castle moat; and some of them seem to have stood on the north side of the gate going into the field in which the castle stands, and perhaps, some of them in the field where the well is, not far from the river.

The castle was afterwards dismantled by Thomas, Earl of Thanet, in the year 1685. Its necessity as a keep had ceased to exist, and so he unroofed it, and taking possession of the lead which was worth something in those days, and all other valuables, left the castle a ruin. After this, in the estimation of the inhabitants, it was little more than "a heap of stones," and became, henceforth, a quarry from which stones were taken for building purposes on the estates of the lord of the manor. Hence, there may be seen at the present day, stones built into the walls and door ways of cow houses, which by their chiselled work, shew their former relation to the castle. Some of the men and women, however, of the last generation saw the stones carted away from the ruin with regret. In our day, the work of further demolition, except that which is the work of time, has ceased. Time, however, is an invisible but constant destroyer; and we cannot but be in sympathy with the lines of Wordsworth's dream of its restoration. He says:

> "How glad Pendragon – though the sleep
> Of years be on her! – she shall reap
> A taste of this great pleasure viewing,
> As in a dream her own renewing."*

We wonder whether this dream will ever become a reality. A reality such as this castle was is impossible; neither would it be

---

*From song at the feast at Brougham Castle

desirable. The ruined stronghold reminds us more forcibly than any other object of the dark ages. Mr. Froude, in his able history, recognises church bells as "the peculiar creation of the medieval age." Bell music, however, has a place, and a charming place in our social life to-day which we should not like to part with. Whereas a feudal stronghold is an anachronism in the age in which we live, and whilst it suggests the cavalcade and the chase, it has another side, and tells of unsettled times, of strife, of lawlessness, of insecurity of life and property, and of the thraldom of the people. Pendragon Castle, which seems to sigh for restoration, rebuilt, and the abode of domestic comfort, such as every truly English home is, would be a splendid crown to its dark and sullen history. And the flag which I saw last summer floating over Appleby Castle, would look equally well floating over one of the restored towers of its sister at Pendragon.

We learn from Machell's MSS. that in 1664 Robert Braithwaite, gentleman, lived at Pendragon Castle, four years after its restoration, and that his wife threw herself off the top of Pendragon Castle, and destroyed her life. We also learn from the Kirkby Stephen church register that in the year 1648 there was buried at Kirkby Stephen Richard Darby, slain by Robert Atkinson, Bluegrass, Mallerstang, and that he slew him in the next bottom close, above Pendragon Castle, on Lord's day in the afternoon. Tradition says that the occasion was a duel, and the weapon used, a sword.

So far as I can learn this is all we know of Pendragon Castle, the foundation stones of which have for so many centuries listened to the babbling waters of the Eden. "I have seen, says the ancient bard of Mallerstang, the walls of Pendragon, but they were desolate. The music had resounded in the halls; but the voice of its people is heard no more. The stream of Eden had removed from its place, by the fall of the walls. There the thistle shook its lovely head. The moss whistled in the wind. The fox looked from the windows, and the rank grass of the wall waved round his head. Desolate is the dwelling of Pembroke; silence is in the house of her Fathers!"* The desolation here referred to has been the source of poetic inspiration to many, from one of which I will make a selection. It is from an old MS. book written by Mr. Garthwaite, who was a schoolmaster in Mallerstang 60 years ago. The poem is signed H. H.

> In a fair vale where sinuous Eden rolls,
> The vestige of an ancient castle stands;
> The asylum of him whose name it bears,
> When civil discord raged within this land.
>
> Oft has this lofty dome re-echoed back
> The clarion's sound; delight of martial minds.
> Within these walls has once been hung
> Such tapestry as adorns a Prince's court.
> Its tables oft have groaned with massy plate;
> And sumptuous feasts prepared for purpled guests.
> Oft has the shining goblet graced the board
> Filled with the liquor of Hesperian fruit.
> Embossed in gold, here, forms of heroes stood,
> Whose valiant feats the sculptured metal told.
> Helmets and spears torn from the conquered foe
> The boasted trophies of these martial knights
> In this grey dome once cast an awful glare.

---

*From Garthwaite's MSS. composed or copied by Fawcett Hunter, of Fell End, Ravenstonedale, dated 1797.

> But ah the fate of sublunary things,
> That lofty pile with turrets in the clouds
> whose well cemented walls thickness immense,
> And sullen doors on massy pillars hung,
> That op'ning jarred harsh discord to the ear
> Could bid defiance to the strongest foe,
> And all the battering engines of the age,
> Now falls a victim to all-conquering time.
> Bleak winter's howling blasts of wind and rain
> Each after each succeeding to the change,
> Compel at last these adamantine walls,
> To shudder down loud thundering to the moon.

I shall now call your attention to the Episcopal Chapel in this township. That the building is ancient is unquestionable, but the date of its erection I cannot learn. Miss Fawcett, in a valuable communication which I have received from her on the subject, says: "I have heard my father [the late Rev. J. Fawcett] say that he believed it was built about 1311." That would be in the reign of Edward II., when Robert de Clifford, who was afterwards slain in the battle of Bannockburn, was the lord of the manor. Canon Simpson, it seems to me, gives the obvious reason of the original erection of the chapel. He says: "Owing to the distance of the parish church, provision was, no doubt, made at Mallerstang, as was usual in such outlying places, to have prayers said in some convenient place by a layman; the clergyman of the parish, himself, attending on certain special occasions to preach a sermon or administer the holy communion. The building was very probably used on week days as a schoolroom, and the prayers said by the schoolmaster." In confirmation of the foregoing, as it affects modern days, Miss Fawcett has informed me that her father had told her that Dr. Robinson not unfrequently sent him over from Ravenstonedale, on a Sunday, some time before he was ordained, to read the prayers and a homily in the chapel here.

Over the porch of the door of the chapel, there used formerly to be a stone with this inscription: "*This chapel was new repayred and covered with blew slates, in 1768.*" From this we infer that the roof was thatched before; indeed of this there is undoubted evidence. Beneath this stone there was another, which the wind blew down some years ago, and was replaced by the Rev. R. Robinson, the late incumbent, when he likewise re-slated the roof on the front side of the chapel, and took down and rebuilt the east wall, at his own cost. The present stone bears exactly the same inscription as the old one, and is as follows: "This Chapple of Mallerstang, after it had layne ruinous and decayed some 50 or 60 years, was newe repayred by the Lady Anne Clifford, Countesse Dowager of Pembroke, Dorsett, and Montgomery, in the year 1663; who also endowed the same with lands, which she purchased in Cawtley near Sedbergh to the yearly value of eleven pounds for ever."

We learn from this that "the Chapel had layne ruinous and decayed some 50 or 60 years." Probably this was largely owing to the unsettled state of things during the Reformation. Ecclesiastically, things had got out of gear. The old order had not yet changed, giving place to the new. Meanwhile, the condition of the people must have been sad in the extreme. There was no other place of worship for them to go to, and they must have been, in the language of scripture, as "sheep not having a shepherd." And all honour to Lady Anne, Countess of Pembroke, that she pitied the destitute condition of the people here by restoring the Chapel, and making provision for the permanent settlement of a minister, who should conduct divine service and teach the children to read and write; and in those days, when there was no School Board as you have to-day, such a provision was a great boon. The original deed, under the hand of the Countess of Pembroke, now in the possession of the Atkinson family at Dale Foot, is as follows:

"Whereas I lately purchased certain lands in Cawtley near Sedbergh in the County of York, to the yearly value of £11 or thereabouts which lands I have given unto, and settled upon the Chapel of Mallerstang in the County of Westmorland for ever, for and to the use and maintenance of a reader to read divine service, and to teach and instruct the children of the dale of Mallerstang aforesaid to read and write, which charge hath been and is still diligently and carefully performed by Rowland Wright, clerk, to the general good satisfaction of the neighbourhood there; and my desire is and I do hereby recommend the same to such of my heirs as shall succeed me in my lands of inheritance in the said County of Westmorland, and to any others whom it may concern that the said Rowland Wright may be continued in the said charge during his life, and enjoy the yearly profits of the said lands, and other the appurtenances belonging to the said Chapel of Mallerstang, he behaving himself (as he hath hitherto done) without any just cause of exception.

"Anne Pembroke,
"Brougham Castle, this 22 of Novr., 1667.

"Signed, sealed and delivered in the presence of
 "Robert Braithwaite,
 "Geo. Sedgwick,
 "Edmond Harker."

The Rowland Wright mentioned aforesaid, I am inclined to think, was the first one appointed under the new order of things, and that, too, after a lengthened interval of pastoral neglect. And

I am also inclined to think that the appointment was made by Lady Anne, and that the endowment of £11 was a subsequent provision towards his support.

I learn from Mr. Garthwaite's papers that in the year 1671 Robert Moore was appointed minister. He was, I should suppose, the immediate successor of Rowland Wright, whose name is mentioned in the aforesaid deed of endowment dated 1667. And it may be interesting to you to know that the following inscription was on the pulpit in the Mallerstang Chapel:

ROBERT MOORE scripsit 1691.

"And Ezra the scribe stood upon a pulpit of wood which he made for preaching." – Neh. viii. 4.

"And he read in the Book of the Law of God distinctly, and gave the sense and caused them to understand the reading." – Neh. viii.8.

Robert Moore, minister, came anno 1671.

This pulpit was replaced by a pulpit and reading-desk made in the year 1798, and which is the one, I presume, now in use.

I have also the following list through the kindness of Miss Fawcett. It is headed, "A book of yearly wages payable to the Chapel of Mallerstang, written by Mr. Robert Moore, June the 15th, 1672," as follows:

OUTHGILL.	s.	d.	SHORTHGILL.	s.	d.
Henry Garthwaite	1	8	Thos. Knwestubb and John his Brother	1	2
Henry Hebden	1	2	Paul Knewstubb	2	10
Thos. Fothergill	1	8	Widow Turner	1	1
John Atkinson	1	1	Thos. Newstubb, Ralph Shaw, and Lionel Turner	1	1
Gabl. Fothergill	1	0			
Henry Shaw	1	1			
Thos Wright	1	8			
	9	4		6	2

MALLERSTANG FOREST

*Castlethwaite.

	s.	d.
Richard Fothergill and Thos. Whitfield	0	8
Thos. Ward	1	2
John Shaw	0	2
Mr. Robt. Braithwaite	2	0
John Fothergill	1	8
Geo. Harrison	0	6
	6	1

Southwaite.

Thos. Waller	1	1
James Fothergill	0	4
John Fothergill	2	2
Thos. Knewstubb	1	0
Michael Fothergill	1	2
Edwd. Fothergill	0	7
The tenement let to Hy. Hugh Fothergill and Wm. Fothergill	1	8
	8	0

Hanging Lund.

Henry Shaw	2	4
Jno. Knewstubb	1	4
Rowland Fothergill	2	4
	6	0

Deep Gill.

W. Birbeck	0	10
Thos. Wharton	0	10
Jeffrey Fothergill	0	10
Brian Hugginson	1	2
	3	8

Sand Pot.

Widow Wharton	1	5
Geo. Hanson	0	
Thos. Dent	1	
Widow Wharton	1	4
John Wharton	1	0
	5	1

Aisgill.

	s.	d.
Henry Whitfield	0	8
Thos. Whitfield, jnr.	1	0
Henry Shaw	1	6
W. Whitfield	0	4
Richard Shaw	1	6
Matt. Whitfield	0	8
	5	8

Elmgill.

Thos. Tunstall	2	0
Edward Shaw	0	10
W. Shearman	0	10
John Shaw	1	8
Rd. Tunstall	0	8
Robert Shaw	0	8
	6	8

Hazelgill.

W. Gibson	1	0
Robert Shaw	1	0
John Hugginson	1	0
Thos. Tunstall	1	0
W. Dent	1	6
Widow Birtal	1	6
	7	0

Anger Holme.

Widow Shaw	0	10
Adam Shaw	2	0
Anth. Shaw	3	4
	6	2

---

* see Appendix, p. 121, for note on derivation of this, and some of the other names.

Dr. Burn says: "The ancient salary of the chapel was about £3 10s a year." And the foregoing amounts to about that sum, commenced, no doubt, by certain payments which landowners in the dale had agreed to make when the chapel was founded, and Canon Simpson is of opinion that the original list may possibly be found in the Registry at Carlisle, and would most likely give us the date of the present foundation of the chapel. Here, I may add, that there are those hearing me who a few years ago saw a copy of such a list signed by Robert Hunter, avowedly taken from a list much older. I have endeavoured to unearth it, but have been unsuccessful. I fear it has been destroyed.* It would appear from this that we cannot trace the subscriptions to the minister earlier than 1513. Still there is nothing in Robert Hunter's testimony to discredit the possible existence of an earlier list. The subscriptions of the people continued until the year 1810, except that they had diminished with the increase of the chapel endowments. In the Terrier of the chapel lands I find the following: "Item: The inhabitants of Mallerstang pay yearly to the Curate for his use the sum of two pounds seventeen shillings and eleven pence." This is the last record I possess of any contributions being raised by the people. However, the minister does not seem to have suffered on that account, for whilst Rowland Wright had eleven pounds a year plus the people's three pounds ten shillings, the Rev. Jeffery

---

* Since delivering the above I have had the good fortune to meet with another copy of the list of wages payable to the minister, of the same date, in the possession of Mr. Thos. Blades. His copy, however, has, in addition to the list, the following valuable note: "I have also a similar account by a Mr Wright," [Mr. Moore's predecessor, I judge, Mr. Rowland Wright] "dated October, 1669. In both accounts there seems to be a reference to an account, dated October, 1543.-I am, yours, &c.,
1814.   ROBERT HUNTER."

Bowness, in whose time the Terrier of 1810 was made out, received altogether ninety-four pounds, taxes included.

In 1867, the date of the last Terrier, there is no record of subscriptions; but I read: "These three estates," at Cawtley, Garsdale, and Sedbergh, the combined rents of which amounted to £157, "constitute the whole of the property belonging to the living of Mallerstang. They are free from tithes, rent charges, and all payments whatsoever." And the present provision for your minister in this year, 1882, is, I understand, much better, which is as it should be; inasmuch as the wise man says, "Better is the end of a thing than the beginning thereof."

In the year 1670 Archbishop Sheldon addressed a circular letter to all the bishops of his province, "commanding them to take notice of all Nonconformists, holders, frequenters, maintainers, and abettors of conventicles, especially of preachers or teachers in them; and of the places where they were held: ever keeping a more watchful eye over the cities and great towns, from whence the mischief is for the most part derived unto the lesser villages and hamlets," &c. Canon Simpson informs me that in the year 1676, after the issue of Archbishop Sheldon's letter, the following names were returned from Mallerstang as amongst those who obstinately refuse or wholly absent themselves from the Communion of the Church of England at such times as by law they are required:

> Thom. Wright, and Dorothy his wife.
> J. O. Knewstubb.
> Hen. Whitfield, jun., and his wife.
> Elizth. Grosedale.
> John Shaw, and Agnes his wife.
> Thos. Knewstubb, and Elizth. his wife.
> Wm. Shaw, Cocklake.

The foregoing were Nonconformists. Where they met for worship we know not, though the fact, could it be ascertained, would doubtless be interesting to you. We need not be surprised to learn that there were Nonconformists here; they were at that time numerous in the adjoining dale of Ravenstonedale, where they enjoyed the ministry of the Rev. Christopher Jackson, of Magdl. Coll., Camb., who had been ejected from the Church at Crosby Garrett. Calamy tells us in his Nonconformists' memorial, "that he lived meanly upon a little estate in the parish of Ravistonedale, preaching occasionally." He adds: "Some minister who had conformed once telling him that he had a bare coat, he made this answer, 'If his coat was bare, it was not turned.'" This dry and pithy retort is in itself characteristic of the Ravenstondale people. From the fact that there was considerable intercourse between the two dales, and that the names of Mallerstang in the foregoing list are identical with those of Ravenstonedale, I think it likely that they were in deep sympathy with each other on this question. Morover, at that time Philip, fourth Lord Wharton, was living at Wharton Hall, just beyond the boundary of your dale towards Kirkby Stephen; and it is known to most of you that he was a distinguished Nonconformist. It is not my business or intention to enter upon the controversies of those sad and troubled times, except that I think it only fair to add that whilst the endeavour of the heads of the Church of England was then to make the gate of admission to the Church as strait as they could, the desire is now to make it as wide as possible.

The following is a list of the ministers of whom we have any record:

| Rowland Wright. | Clerk. | 1667. |
| Robert Moore. | | 1671. |

After this we come to a gap which, for want of information, we cannot fill up.

Thomas Gascoigne.	Clerk.	1740.
Lancelot Pattison.	Clerk.	1754.
Jeffery Bowness.		1761.
John Bird.	Clerk.	
Wm. Bird.	do.	
John Fawcett.	do.	1819.
Robert Robinson.	do.	1844.
Wm. Alnwick.	do.	1878.

The Rev. R. Robinson, your last incumbent, was known to myself. He was a kindly man when I made his acquaintance. He once informed me that in the year 1835 he was the Wolverhampton Lecturer, which was certainly an honour. He was a clergyman of the old school, who took an interest in the secular as well as spiritual interest of his charge. He never taught the day school, but paid a schoolmaster from £25 to £30 a year to do it for him, which was supplemented, I understand, for some time by a committee who, in order to secure the services of a duly-qualified man, made it up to £50 by subscription. He was the son of the well known Rev. Dr. Robinson, who conducted a high class school in Ravenstonedale, and of whom the Bishop of Carlisle (Bishop Law) said to your late minister: "Your father, by his college school, kept a light for the Church of England in your part of the county of Westmorland which, but for him, would have been in a dark and destitute condition." Your minister was born and brought up in Ravenstonedale, and for his native parish he ever cherished, I can testify, almost a romantic love – everything and everybody from Ravenstonedale pleased him; and, at his express wish, his remains now lie in the churchyard there.

It would not be in good taste for me to characterise your present incumbent, except to say that in all my relations with him I have ever found him courteous and gentlemanly.

Soon after the appointment of your present incumbent, the chapel, which had got out of repair, was renovated and reopened on the 8th of May, 1879, after it had been closed for six months. The pulpit at the north side of the Communion table was lowered, and the reading desk removed to the south side. The Communion rails were new. A new floor was laid down. A gallery at the west end was taken away. A heating apparatus was put in; also new outer and inner doors. A vestry was made and suitably furnished, and all at the expense of Sir J. H. Tufton, now Lord Hothfield, the patron of the living. And may your church ever remain, what I believe it is to-day, a source of bright, gospel light.

The following are the sources of the chapel's endowment:

1. An estate, the original endowment of the chapel, situated at a place called Wards in Cautley, in the parish of Sedbergh and county of York, given by Lady Ann, Countess of Pembroke, &c., the rent of which is £32.*

2. An estate called Little Town, in Garsdale, in the parish of Sedbergh, from money given by the Earl of Thanet, 1714, and Queen Anne's bounty. Rent, £65.

3. An estate, situated at Gill, in the parish of Sedbergh, from money (£400) given by the late Lady Gower, 1772, and added to the bounty of Queen Anne. Rent, £60.

It is the opinion of Canon Simpson that no regular incumbent was appointed until after the grant of Queen Anne's bounty; before that it was a chapel of ease to the church at Kirkby Stephen.

---

*The above is taken from the terrier of the chapel lands, 1867.

From the same authority I also learn that the three townships of Mallerstang, Naitby, and Wharton formed one of the four divisions, each of which was entitled to appoint a churchwarden of the parish church of Kirkby Stephen, and so long as church rates were levied, Mallerstang had to contribute its share to the mother church. It still pays tithes to the vicar of Kirkby Stephen, bestowed originally by St. Mary's Abbey, York, and was commuted in the year 1842 at £62 per annum. There are no rectorial tithes, and never were, which proves that the land in Mallerstang was generally pasture and meadow.

Seventy years ago, the inhabitants, finding it a long way to carry their dead to Kirkby Stephen, petitioned the Bishop to consecrate a burial ground near their own place of worship. The first interment was that of Margaret Moore, and took place July 15th, 1813. She was aged 82. Through the kindness of the vicar, the Rev. W. Alnwick, I have looked through the register, and have been surprised at the evidence which it furnishes of the longevity of the people. I select one page, and take the names *seriatim* as they occur, *i.e.,* in the exact order in which the burials took place.*

1823.

Dec. 28.	Buried	Mary Ward of Outhgill. Aged 91.
Dec 31.	Buried	Elizabeth Brunskill of Cocklake. Aged 86.

1824.

Feb. 4.	Buried	Margaret, widow of Hugh Blenkhorn. She died, in Ingram in the parish of Aisgarth and county of York. Aged 87.

---

* Here I should say that I received the first intimation of this page from the late Mr. G. Blades. This family have kept a private register of the burials in Mallerstang Churchyard from the beginning.

Mar. 7.	Buried	Richard Fothergill, late of Sand Pot. He died at Southwaite. Aged 86,
1824.		
June 9.	Buried	Buried John Metcalfe of Aisgill, late at Hazlegill. Aged 87.
June 16.	Buried	Robert Atkinson of Blue grass. Aged 92.
June 22.	Buried	Anna Rennison, Cocklake. Aged 76.
Aug. 11.	Buried	Mary Brown, Tarn House, Ravenstonedale. Aged 78

There is a sense of completeness that the graveyard God's acre, as the Saxons called it – surrounds the chapel. It obviates the necessity of funeral journeys to Kirkby Stephen through all kinds of rough weather, which the late Geo. Blades told me he was old enough to remember; and, moreover, it is a satisfaction to you to have the remains of your dear ones lying in your midst.

From the recollections of inhabitants I learn that the chapel door was of double oak, very massive, with a sort of ring for a handle or sneck. The windows were glazed in lead, with iron bars across to protect them. Inside the chapel there was a gallery at the west end. The seats were made of oak, and some of the backs were beautifully carved. The pulpit and reading desk were likewise of oak. There is a chalice and plate that were presented by the Rev. W. Williamson, Vicar of Kirkby Stephen, and likewise the large Bible and Prayer Book used in church. In the bottom entrance of the church there used to be a stone let into the wall, with a round hole hewn out of the stone, with an outlet to pour the water out that had been used at baptism.

The half of the incumbent's fees for burials, christenings, and churchings, used to be claimed by the vicar of Kirkby Stephen; and at the death of every landowner 8s. 6d. was paid to the vicar as a mortuary fee. Every Easter Tuesday the vicar of Kirkby Stephen preached in the chapel, and, after service, examined the registers and received the fees, and afterwards the incumbent and churchwardens dined with him at the King's Head, Outh-gill. The vicar of Kirkby Stephen provided four bottles of wine yearly for the Sacrament. The vicar of Kirkby Stephen sent his clerk every Easter to collect dues, 3d. for every communicant and so many eggs each house, likewise 3d. for every smoke in the farmhouses.

There are three books kept in the iron chest which used formerly to stand in a recess behind the pulpit. The Registers commence in the year 1730. There used to be a library belonging to the Chapelry of Mallerstang. The books were well bound, and had a paper inside with *Mallerstang Chapel Library* written upon it. The subjects generally treated upon Theology. The burial ground was consecrated by Bishop Goodenough on the 9th of July in the year 1813. The school was in an upstairs room in the chapel. The room is small, and badly lighted. Miss Fawcett says in her recollections: "In the year 1819 my father was appointed curate of Mallerstang at a stipend of £50 a year, and out of this small income he had to teach the school. Here many of the old dalesmen received a plain, practical education, and had instilled into them the principles of honesty and uprightness, under his care. And many of the old farmers will tell you with pride that the new system of education, with their Board Schools and new – fangled ways, are not able to turn out such scholars as parson Fawcett did." From a subsequent communication, Miss Fawcett also says: "The tables, with the Commandments and Lord's Prayer and Creed, over the communion table, were painted and re-lettered by John Moore, of Mallerstang, the father to the present Moores of Ravenstonedale. I believe the people used formerly to sit on benches in chapel. When my father was curate, the chapel was reseated with pews. There used to be a gallery at the west end of the chapel, but the hand of change has been laid on the old building, and all these, like the good old times of former years, have disappeared. The parish clerk was John Fothergill, or rather John at Green (for he hardly knew his own name), and old Joe Atkinson, the sexton. These were two notable characters, in their day, in the dale; and when old Atkinson had to leave his house at Shor Gill to come to Outh-gill, a distance under three hundred yards, he told my father he could not imagine what he had done that he should be transported. Such was the love they had for their old homesteads. The late Bishop, Dr. Waldegrave, preached in Mallerstang Chapel in August, 1867, to a crowded congregation. His subject was the brazen serpent, and his sermon will long live in the remembrance of the people. The present Bishop, Dr. Goodwin, visited Mallerstang in 1874, but has never preached in the chapel. He expressed himself much pleased with the simplicity and romantic beauty of the valley."

LECTURE III.

It is not my intention in these lectures to enter with anything like detail upon the forest laws. You will see that it is sufficient for my purpose to say that they were framed by William the Conqueror, and adopted soon after the Norman Conquest. The whole of this part of the county was given to Ranulph de Meschines, one of the knights of William the Conqueror; and the laws of the forest here were no doubt modelled on those of his august master. Nicholson and Burn, in their "History of Westmorland," say: "Also in the tenures of many of the manors, there were certain services respecting the forests; as to keep airey of hawks for the lord's use, to herd the lord's hogs during mastage season, to watch with nets or dogs at such a station." Whether such oversight of game was a condition of tenure here or not I cannot say, although the fine of £20 each, levied on Thomas Knewstubb and others, for killing a deer in the forest of Mallerstang so late as the year 1665, and to which I called your attention in the first lecture, was very severe, when you think of the much higher value of money in those days. Happily, however, that period has gone, and although your forest has never been disforested, I understand, practically it makes no difference to you. There is no one living who ever remembers to have seen a deer on the hills; and the lesser game also have disappeared before the advance of cultivation. Indeed the very term forest, which at one time gave your dale its pre-eminent distinction, has disappeared. Who would ever think now-a-days of speaking of going to Mallerstang forest? Invariably it would be Mallerstang, or, if speaking in the dialect, Mauston. Those of you who have not read Whitaker's "History of Richmondshire," will be glad to peruse the following extract, which bears directly upon the forest which once existed here. He says: "After all the encroachments of cultivation in Swaledale since the time of Doomesday, much forest ground remained, connected perhaps with the largest tract of waste in South Britain. The forests of the Earl of Richmond, besides that of Wensleydale, comprehended that part of Stainmore included within the parish of Bowes, all Applegarth, and Arkengarthdale. These were afterwards reduced to the New Forest of later date, as it name imports, than the rest, and lying wholly in the parish of Kirkby Ravenswath. North-west was Lune [Lunds] Forest, and beyond Stainmore and Mallerstang in Westmorland. Southward lay Bishopdale Chase connected with Longstrathdale in the West Riding, and all were ranged by herds of wild deer, the noblest chase of our ancient hunters, whose pursuits were certainly the best preparatives for war both to the knight and his steed. Of these the New Forest alone subsists even in name. The Duke of Leeds is ranger." Here I should add that up to within the last few years the sum of 11s. 2d. was paid annually out of the poor rates to George Lane Fox, Esq., called "the Duke of Leeds' money." For some time I have been unable to learn its meaning or design; the foregoing extract makes it clear. It was originally a fine paid to the ranger of the forest. There is one paragraph more from Whitaker with which I should like to furnish you, as it is decidedly to the point. He continues: "But of this wild extent of waste, a great part becoming the property of the Crown, and in consequence liable to neglect and depredation, Swaledale, which was carefully protected by the Wharton family, became the last refuge of the persecuted deer, which remained in considerable numbers northwards from Muker as late as the year 1725. With the deer vanished their ancient refuge and browse, the woods which were gradually consumed by the smelt mills, for after the warm and sheltered gills were stripped, the stags pined for want of their accustomed winter food, of which many died, while the rest fell an easy prey to poachers. After the nobler pursuit had ceased, hawking and netting of grouse was in use in the year 1725, when shooting-flying was introduced to the great astonishment of the dalesmen."

Although Mallerstang is a township or chapelry of Kirkby Stephen it is distinct as a manor. The Court book now in the possession of the bailiff, Mr. Thomas Blades, which contains the entries of the admittances made from time to time of the tenants of the lord of the manor into the estates of Mallerstang, bears date on its first page, 1742. The three or four pages following are taken up with the laws of the manor. These laws are the result of a dispute which Earl Sackville had with his tenants in Westmorland about their fines after the death of the Earl Thomas. After a long contest in Chancery, a trial at bar in 1739 was directed to be, by a special jury of the County of Middlesex – [in which eleven witnesses were produced by the tenants from Westmorland whose ages together amounted to a thousand years] – on the two following issues, viz,:—

1. Whether by the custom of the respective manors of Brougham, Appleby, Brugh under Stainmore, Pendragon, Kirkby Stephen, Kings' Meaburn, Langton, Mallerstang, Knock, Sowerby, East Stainmore, South Stainmore, Scattergate and Burrel,

Woodside, Moorhouses, Burgate, Burgh Over, and Burgh Nether, on the death of the last general admitting lord, a reasonable fine to be assessed at the will of the lord, not exceeding two years' value be payable; or any other and what fine?

2. Whether by custom of the said manors, on the death or alienation of the tenant, a reasonable fine to be assessed at the will of the lord, not exceeding two years' value, be payable, or any other and what fine? The verdict of the jury was that such fines according to the yearly value were not payable. But that first, by custom of the same manors, and every of them, on the death of the last general admitting lord, a fine to be assessed at the will of the lord, not exceeding ten pence for every penny old rent, commonly called a tenpenny fine, is payable; and second, that by custom of the said manors and every of them, on the death or alienation of the tenant, a reasonable fine to be assessed at the will of the lord not exceeding seventeen penny fine is payable. And the same was decreed accordingly by the Lord Chancellor Hardwick. And by consent as to other matters in dispute it was referred to Robert Fenwick and Joseph Taylor, Esquires, and such other third person as they should appoint to settle the same: who made an award, and the same was inserted accordingly in the decree." Then follow the manorial laws which have been in operation ever since the year 1739.

1. That the tenants hold their tenements according to the ancient custom of tenant right, and as customary estates of inheritance, descended from ancestor to heir under certain ancient yearly rents, and such general and dropping fines [fines of sale] as are settled and ascertained by the order in this cause.

2. By the custom of the said manors upon all admittances where the ancient rent exceeds ls. 3d., and no more is payable to the steward for every single admittance: and where one tenant

hath several admittances at the same court, and the ancient rent of any one of them exceeds ls., then 3s. is payable for the first admittance, and 6d. for every other: where the ancient rent doth exceed ls. then ls. only is payable for every single admittance; and where one tenant hath several admittances at the same court, and the ancient rent of one of them exceeds ls., in such case ls. only is payable for the first and 6d. for every other.

3. That the tenants have a right to open quarries within their own estates, or in the wastes of the manor, and get stones for building or repairing their houses or fences, or other necessary uses upon their estates, without licence of the lord or of his steward; but may not open quarries, or get stone out of quarries in lease or opened by the lord without such licence.

4. That the tenants have right to cut up, take and carry away turf, peat, heath, furze and bracken or fern, upon the wastes for fuel and thatching without such licence.

5. That the tenants have right to plow and make such husbandry of their lands as they think fit, without such license.

6. That the tenants have a right to lease or demise their tenements for any term not exceeding three years.

7. That all absolute sales or alienations ought to be by deed poll, or indented; and the same to be presented at the next court, in order for the purchaser to be admitted on payment of droping fines, "Femes covert" interested in lands alienated to be examined privately by the steward.

8. That the tenants may mortgage for any term not exceeding three years without licence or fine; but when the mortgage(e) is admitted he shall pay a droping fine [i.e., the fine of sale].

9. That the tenants may without license or fine exchange lands lying intermixed in common fields for lands of equal value in the same manor; so it be with the approbation of the lord or his steward.

10. That the tenants may cut down and sell underwood growing in their respective tenements: and may cut down and use any other wood or timber for repair of their tenements, hedge boot, plough boot, cart boot, estovers, and other necessary uses, provided the same be set out by the lord or his steward (the same to be without fee) in 20 days after request in writing, attested by one witness, and if not set out within that time the tenants may cut down and use the same.

11. That the lord may fell timber provided he leave sufficient for repairs, necessary boots, and estovers.

Some of the foregoing laws are still in force, and others are obsolete, being out of harmony with the spirit of the present age. There is no danger, however, of these being revived under the wise and liberal rule of the present lord of the manor. In the year 1808 the tenants of Ravenstonedale purchased their freedom of the lord of the manor, and perhaps I may be excused for suggesting that the tenants of Mallerstang should, with the consent of the lord of the manor, imitate their example. Feudalism rendered its service in its day, but that day has gone, and all the influences of our age are working in an opposite direction. The fines of the lord of the manor amount to about £45 per annum. His Court is held at Kirkby Stephen once a year, and is presided over by his steward. One jury – "homage jury" – is held for Mallerstang, composed as far as can be of owners of property in Mallerstang. One jury also is held for Kirkby Stephen, and a grand jury is constituted out of the two, Mallerstang and Kirkby Stephen being represented in equal proportions, *i.e.,* six for each. At this Court admittances are made either by descent or alienation, *i.e.,* by sale. From the Court book I learn that up to within the last few years, when an encroachment of the common had been made by one of the tenants, the lord's rent upon it, together with grassam and joist, were determined upon. In the present day no such encroachments are allowed. It is entirely beyond the scope of these lectures to give any lengthy extracts from the Court book. Still it may interest you to hear the first few entries. After the following intimation – "May 6th, 1743. After the rental in the first page was signed by the jury, the verdict was delivered to the steward, and the following tenants were admitted tenants" -we read: "Mr. Lancelot Pattinson, son and heir of Thomas Pattinson, Esqre., deceased, was admitted tenant of several messauges and tenements, with the finable rent of £3 5s. 2d., grassam and joist, £11s. 4d. (2) William Hutchinson was admitted tenant by deed of purchase from Lancelott Hutchinson of a messuage and tenement with the finable rent of £1 13s. 4½d., grassam and joist, £0 3s. 4½d." (3) Ralph Milner was admitted tenant by deed of purchase from John Bousfield of a messuage and tenement with the finable rent of 12s., grassam and joist 6d. (4) John Bainbridge was admitted tenant by a mortgage deed from Mary Rudd of a messuage and tenement with the finable rent of 18s. 0½d., grassam and joist 3s. 3¾d.

The entries are all of a very business-like character. The farms are usually given in case of admittances. Admittances usually specify the name of the farm or farms. The originals with the signatures, and in many instances more amplified particulars, are in the possession of the lord of the manor. Interspersed with the decisions of the Court revised lists occur of those who were liable to pay rent to the lord of the manor. The first in the book is dated October 23, 1754, and is as follows:

"The finable rent the Tenants were admitted tenants to their estates with, to the Right Honble Sacville Earl of Thanet at a Court held the 23rd day of October 1754 for assessing the general fine by William Gorst Gentleman steward. Also the grassam and joyst due out of each Tenement.

MALLERSTANG FOREST

	Finable Rent				Grassam & Joist			
	£	s	d	Pk	£	s	d	Pk
John Wharton	1	14	2½		0	4	3	
Thomas Dent	0	7	11½		0	1	7	
Philip Wharton	0	9	3		0	1	0½	
Thomas Ward	0	11	7½		0	1	6	
Thomas Ward	0	3	40 0 6					
Thos. Gascoigne Clerk	0	4	7		"	"	6½	
Isabel Wharton	0	10	0½		0	1	4	
James Fothergill	0	2	8		"	"	4	
Richard Morland	0	6	6½	2	"	"	11	
John Fothergill	0	2	5		"	"	3¾	
Thomas Ward	0	11	0½		"	1	4½	
Lancelot Pattison, clerk	3	5	2½		"	7	1¾	
Richard Fothergill	"	"	4		"	"	"	
John Hutchinson	"	1	1		"	"	1	
Agnes Whitfield	"	"	1"		"	"	"	
Thomas Garthwaite	"	"	3		"	"	0½	
Edward Metcalf	"	"	1½		"	"	"	
Anthony Ward	"	3	10½		"	"	6¼	
Adam Robinson	"	6	4		"	"	9	
John Shaw	"	12	8½		"	"	11½	
John Metcalf	"	6	4½		"	"	6½	
Eleanor Robinson	1	6	9	2	"	3	4	
Matthew Robinson	"	6	4½		"	"	6½	
William Hutchinson	1	13	4½			3	4½	
Agnes Winn	"	17	6½			1	9	2
Joseph Fothergill	"	6	4½				10½	
William Fothergill	"	6	4				10½	
William Grainger	"	8	8				8½	
John Fothergill		5	4				5½	
Anthony Fothergill		"	1				"	
John Atkinson	0	9	0½		0	0	8½	
Richard Dixon	0	1	6		"	"	1½	
Isaiah Fothergill			1½		"	"	"	
Richard Balderstone	"	5	4		"	"	11½	
Wm. Guy	"	9	1½		"	1	6¾	
John Steward	0	19	11			2	8¼	
John Bainbridge	"	18	0½			3	3¾	
Jane Metcalfe	"	"	4½			"	0½	
Margret Ellens	"	"	3				0½	
Thomas Whitfield		10	5			1	4½	

MALLERSTANG FOREST 55

	Finable Rent				Grassam & Joist			
	£	s	d	Pk	£	s	d	Pk
James Shaw	"	9	8			1	3½	
William Shaw	"	10	2¾			1	3¼	
John Fothergill	"	3	0			"	4½	
John Scaif		4	7				6¾	
Michael Scaif		4	7				6¾	
Henry Hugginson		6	4			"	8½	
John Shaw		1	6			"	1½	
Bell Parkin	1	0	5			1	4½	
Henry Shaw	0	15	0			3	6	
Henry Shaw	0	2	6			0	7	
Elzie. Shaw, jun	0	6	5½		0	1	5½	
John Shaw	0	10	2		0	2	2¾	
Richard Scaif		0	2		"	"	"	
Elizabeth Shaw		"	1		"	"	"	
Mary Ewbank	0	16	2		"	2	11	
Robert Blenkam	0	2	10		"	"	4½	
Ann Cowperthwaite	0	2	4		"	"	5	
Robert Parkin	2	14	5½		"	4	2	
William Parkin	0	5	2¼		0	"	7¾	
Robert Jonson	"	9	3		"	"	11½	
Benjamin Shaw	"	4	6		"	"	5½	
Jonathan Shaw	"	7	6		"	"	10½	
William Winn	1	9	2		"	3	8½	
Thomas Tunstall	0	11	1		"	1	2	
John Tunstall	0	12	6		"	1	1½	
Brian Hugginson	0	15	0		"	2	1½	
Brian Huggin son	0	7	1		"	1	2¾	
Robert Hugginson	0	10	6		"	1	6	
Edward Hazel	0	13	5		"	2	8	
Samuel Shaw	0	9	8		"		10½	

In the foregoing list mention is made of charges in grassom and joiest: the meaning of grassom is grassing upon the common, and joiest agistment or cattle gates; these are not subject to lords' fines. Also the plack is mentioned, a small coin which owing to the diminution in the value of money, has gone entirely out of use, as the farthing is going out of use in our day. Mr. Garthwaite, to whose MSS. I have referred before, copied the following from a

Kendal paper, dated 1813. "Tradition says some brass tokens were coined at Kendal about the year 1656 called placks, and states that three of them were of the value of a halfpenny." On the plack the Reverend W. Thompson has furnished me with the following excellent note. He says "The plack was a copper coin formerly current in Scotland. It was of the value of one-third of an English penny. The word is derived from the French *plaque- a* thin piece of metal. It is of frequent allusion in Scottish litererature. I quote one out of several allusions in Burns:

> "There's ae wee faut they whiles lay to me,
> I like the lasses – Gude forgie me!
> For mony a plack they wheedle frae me,
> At dance or fair."

Another from Anderson's Cumberland ballads:

> "At Carel, when for six pounds ten
> I selt twea Scotty kye,
> They pick'd my pocket i' the thrang,
> And deil a plack had I."

No doubt the name had its origin in Scotland, although it seems to have been locally applied also to the Kendal Tradesmen's brass tokens, a description of several of which is given in Nicholson's "Annals of Kendal." He says (and this agrees with Mr. Garthwaite's extract), "Tradition calls these pieces placks, and it is stated that three of them were of the value of a halfpenny."

The following is the last revised list of tenants given in the Court book, from which you will see that whilst the tenants numbered 70 in 1754 the names numbered 30 in 1880. They are as follows:

MALLERSTANG FOREST 57

	Customary Rent			Grassom and Joist			Free Rent	
	£	s	d	£	s	d	s.	d.
John Grimshaw	2	15	"	"	6	9½	"	"
ditto	2	14	0¼	"	5	11½	"	2
Anthony Metcalf (in trust)	"	18	"	"	2	"	"	"
ditto (in trust)	"	17	0½	"	2	5½	"	1
ditto late Elizh. Cleasby	"	12	6	"	"	7	2	6*
Wm. Cleasby late Anthony Metcalf	2	6	2¾	"	9	2¾	"	"
Thomas Cleasby (Ridding House)	"	1	6	"	"	1½	"	"
Abram Dent late Alice Hunter	"	8	4	"	"	10½	"	"
Abram Dent late Isabella Dent	"	15	2	"	1	11	"	"
George Blades late Peggy Blades	"	5		"	"	6	"	"
George Blades	2	10	5½	"	4	5½	"	"
George Blades late Dixon	"	1	8	"	"	"	"	"
Thos. Blades late Anthony Morland	"	13	5	"	1	11¼	"	"
ditto late Robert Hutchinson	"	11	0	"	1	1½	"	"
ditto late Ann Atkinson	"	5	7	"	"	10	"	"
ditto late Ann Atkinson	1	2	1¾	"	2	9½	"	"
ditto late Ann Garthwaite	"	8	5	"	1	1¼	"	"
Thos. Blades late Peggy Blades	"	7	10½	"	1	0½	"	"
ditto late Joseph Throup	"	"	1	"	"	"	"	"
James Atkinson, late Robert Atkinson	"	"	4	"	"	"	"	"
Henry Walley late Sarah Robinson	1	1	5½	"	2	7½	"	"
Matthew Robinson	1	2	3	"	2	3	"	"
Matthew Metcalf	1	2	10½	"	2	2¾	"	"
Robert Burra late Matthew Thompson	4	5	3¼	"	12	7¼	"	"
ditto late ditto	1	18	"	"	4	3¼	"	1
Robert Fothergill	"	6	4	"	"	10½	"	"
Jane Fawcett ⎱ Mary Fawcett ⎰ late Mary Fawcett	"	"	6	"	"	"	"	"
Jane Fawcett late Mary Fawcett	"	6	6	"	"	10½	"	"
Ann Fawcett	"	5	7¾	"	"	11	"	"
Elizth Fawcett	"	5	7¾	"	"	11	"	"
Mary Fawcett	"	5	7¾	"	"	10½	"	"
Jane Fawcett	"	5	7½	"	"	10	"	"
John Grainger	1	11	"	"	5	9¾	2	6**
Philip Harrison	"	18	1	"	2	3¾	"	"

---

* Incroach
** Pasture Rent.

Agnes Ann Thompson late John Thompson	"	1	6	"	"	1½	"	"
Eleanor Shaw	"	7	6	"	2	2	"	"
Joseph King late Abram Dent	"	"	1	"	"	"	"	"
Thomas Mason late John Dickinson	"	"	3	"	"	"	"	"
Midland Railway Company late George Blades	"	5	"	"	"	"	"	"
ditto late John Grainger	"	3	6	"	"	"	"	"
ditto late John Grimshaw	"	2	1½	"	"	"	"	"
ditto late ditto	"	3	4	"	"	"	"	"
ditto late A.E.M. & J Fawcett	"	1	3	"	"	"	"	"
ditto late Jane Fawcett	"	1	4	"	"	"	"	"
ditto late Anthony Metcalfe	"	1	3	"	"	"	"	"
ditto late ditto	"	2	"	"	"	"	"	"
ditto late Abraham Dent	"	"	1	"	"	"	"	"
ditto late Jane Fawcett	"	"	2	"	"	"	"	"
ditto late Robert Burra (in trust)		1	6	"	"	"	"	"
ditto late A.E.M. & J. Fawcett	"	1	3	"	"	"	"	"

Also amongst the admittances there is one entry which shows that the subject of it must have produced considerable excitement at the time, to draw aside a chronicler who in every other instance is so colourless and indifferent to what is passing. It is this: "At a court holden by adjournment the 21st day of May, 1754. The reason of this court not being kept at the usual time was occasioned by the great contested election for the burrow of Applby betwixt Lord of Thanet and Sir James Lowther, which election continued a month, and at the shutting up of the books Lord of Thanet had a majority of 13 votes." Evidence is furnished here of one of those election struggles which at the time engrossed so much attention, but has long since been forgotten.

The last admittance but one is of Mr. Thomas Blades, dated October 11th, 1882, to the estates of his father, Mr. George Blades, recently deceased. Mr. Thomas Blades also succeeds his brother as* bailiff of the manor, and to his kindness and courtesy I am indebted for much valuable information in these lectures.

The following is a copy of the written record of the admittance into the Court Book, and as it is the last, at this date given, I will furnish it in full:

MANOR OF KIRKBY STEPHEN	The Court Leet, and Court Baron of the Right Honorable Henry James Baron Hothfield of Hothfield, Lord of the said Manor held at the Black Bull Inn Kirkby Stephen within the said Manor on Wednesday the eleventh day of October 1882 by Edward Heelis Esqr Steward of the said Manor

The names of the Jurors to enquire for the Lord of the Manor aforesaid and between Tenant and Tenant for Mallerstang—

Thomas Blades Foreman	John Clark
Robert Fothergill	John Harrison
Abram Dent	John Iveson
Thomas Cleasby	James Savage
John Thompson	Lancelot Fairer
Robert Troughton	John Dodd

Who being sworn and charged, Present and find as follows,

"We the Homage Jury of the Lordship of Mallerstang present and find George Blades deceased, and Thomas Blades his only surviving Son and Customary Heir of All that Messuage and Tenemant consisting of a Dwelling House and Other Out Buildings and several Closes of Land thereto belonging at Angerholme Also a close of Land Called Low Holme part of a Tenement called Ingends containing by estimation four Acres and five perches be the same more or Less

Also a messuage and Tenement Situate and being at Ingheads consisting of a Dwelling House two Barns and several Inclosures of Land with the Apurtenances in Mallerstang within the said Manor of the

---

*See Appendix, page 122.

several yearly Customary Rents of £2 10s. 2d. ls. 8d. and 5s. Grassam and Joist 4s. 5½d. and sixpence and other Dues Duties and Services
Finable Rent £2 l6s. 10d.
Grassam and Joist 4s. 11½d.

THOMAS BLADES Foreman

We also present and find that Matthew Metcalf by Deed dated the 30th day of December 1881 hath Alienated to John Bland Davis all that Messuage and Tenement and several Closes or Inclosures and parcels of Land theirunto Belonging Called Southwaite (formerly Winn's) Also All that Messuage and Tenement and several Closes of Land called Castlethwaite (formerly Ward's) containing all together 42 Acres 1 Rood and 19 Perches or thereabouts, with the Apurtenances in Mallerstang within the Said Manor of the yearly customary Rent of £1 2s. 10½ d. Grassam and Joist 2s. 2¾d. and two Placks and other Dues Duties and Services
Finable Rent £1 2s. 10½ d Placks
Grassam and Joist 2s. 2¾d. 2

THOMAS BLADES Foreman

We now come to the roads. The present road through Mallerstang is modern. It was made under an Act sixth year of George IV., cap. 12, 1825, and was dis-turnpiked a few years since. The course of the old road, and for which I have the authority of the late Mr. Geo. Blades, was as follows. These are his words: "It crossed Hell Bridge out of Yorkshire into Westmorland, over Hell Gill Woad to Woad* End, down Woad Side to Elm Gill. Thence along on the common to Thrang Bridge. Thence along down the

---

*The word " woad" is said to be a corruption of " wold," and on the word wold Webster says in his Dictionary: "Wold, in Saxon, is the same as wald and weald, a wood; somtimes perhaps a lawn or a plain."

fields to Eden. Across the Eden to Shorgill. Thence through the fields to Sand Pot. Thence down the common to Birkett.* Thence across the Eden to Wharton Park." The following is another contribution also on the roads from the same authority; and so quaint and graphic is it that you would be sorry for it to be omitted. He says: "The pack horses used to come into Mallerstang from Cotterdale; they passed a place called Cotter End, across the common, and over Hell Gill Bridge; there they entered Mallerstang, kept on the common until they came to Thrang Bridge. Those that had set out from Grisedale† came across the common until they came to High Shaw Paddock; they then came along some enclosed common; on leaving that enclosed common they entered Mallerstang Common, thence down to Aisgill, and from Aisgill to Thrang‡ Bridge, where the two parties generally met on their way to the Kirkby market with butter in their baskets." Mr. Geo. Blades remembered pack horses going from Swaledale to Kirkby Stephen. He particularly recollected noticing their wooden saddles, on which they tied bags, &c. Here I may remind you that there is still an inn at Kirkby Stephen with the sign of the Pack Horse; and when the Mallerstangians used to go to Kirkby Stephen to be married, the damsels rode on horseback on pillions behind their trusty swains. Also Mr. Blades told me that he remembered "about sixty years ago a Scotch drover came into the township with a herd of Highland cattle. The man, tired, sat down, and the beasts lay around him. On rising to continue his journey he played the bagpipes, and the cattle followed him!"

Whilst we are on this subject of roads, I should add that there was also a road that branched off at Aisgill, and went over Anger

---

* The place where the birch tree grows.

† Grisedale, i.e., Dale of the wild boar.

‡Thrang. The radical meaning of this word is hurrying, pressing.

Holme road, and crossed the boundary over Scarth Nick, thence down the common in Ravenstonedale to Stenners Keugh, joining the old road from Sedbergh to Kirkby Stephen at Street. This road is used occasionally still. The other road from Mallerstang into Ravenstonedale, and of which the writer has in the winter time had troublesome experience, branches off from Pendragon Castle, and passes over Green Law, on to Ash Fell.

Previous to the introduction of railways, the road through Mallerstang was a great and crowded thoroughfare during Brough Hill Fair. It is said that many of the inhabitants of Ravenstonedale used to go there to witness the animated scene – "a miscellaneous panorama of men and things defiling through the dale" – and that they might lose no time, took their knitting with them. Amongst the inhabitants, I am told, there were some thrifty ones, who, eighty years ago, used to go up to Hell Gill Bridge, and set out on tables, nuts, apples, gingerbread, sweeties, &c., to sell to those who were going to or from Brough Hill Fair. At other times, however, the road was sequestered and dangerous for travellers to venture upon, owing to highwaymen – three especially – who lived in the dale. Their names were Ned Ward, a native of the dale, who lived at Farclose House; Riddle, who was a border man; and Brodrick, who seems to have come from Orton. These men seem to have been highwaymen of the magnanimous stamp – that is to say, they would not rob the poor or any of their neighbours; indeed, though their practices were known, they were in a certain sense respected by their neighbours. However, this highway robbery very properly came to an end at last. A robbery had been committed in which these men were implicated. Two officers on horseback went to Shorgill and secured Brodrick. They then went on up the dale, and crossed Thrang Bridge, and entered Ward's house, standing only a short distance beyond it, to apprehend Ward. He was at the time only partly dressed, and asked permission to go up stairs and finish dressing. No sooner was he on the upper storey than he removed the thatch, got out on the roof, descended, leapt on one of the officer's horses, and galloped off. Almost immediately, of course, one of the officers was in full pursuit on the other horse, which was the better of the two. The chase must have been exciting. So Ward galloped down Boggle Green, and finding his pursuer close upon him, leapt from his horse and crossed the Eden. This his pursuer could not do, and so sent a bloodhound in full pursuit. Meanwhile Ward descended the dale, and came to Hall Hill. The dog was now close upon him. This, Scaife, a resident, seeing from his house, sent a lad to him with a thick stick, with which he disabled the dog. Soon afterwards he concealed himself in a coal level, and from thence, when he thought it safe, went to his cousin at Ladfoot. Here he clothed himself, and set out for Newcastle, where he worked for many years in the mines. Mr. "Joe Steel" saw him in Kirkby Stephen long after, an old man; he and his brother Kit were together. Brodrick, who had turned king's evidence, remained in prison for awhile. On regaining his freedom he was an altered man; he became a good and useful member of society. He was a mason by trade, and built Musgrave Bridge, and the portico and stables of the King's Arms, Kirkby Stephen.

Here I must notice the public houses. Outh Gill had an inn twenty years ago. Indeed there had been an inn there from time immemorial, its sign was the King's Head. Cranberry was also a public house thirty years ago; its sign was the Black Bull. The woman who kept it about a hundred years ago was quite a character. Her name was Betsy Ward, though she was usually called "Rapsy Bett." She had never married, I understand; but it is said that when the Scotchmen were driving their cattle and sheep into the Craven districts of Yorkshire, they occasionally put up at her house for the night. When they enquired "Where shall we leave our cattle, missus, what part is yours?" she used to say, standing with her face to the common, and winking as hard as she could, with a peculiarity that belonged to her, while pointing to the common, "Put them where you like; all that I see is my own." Such an anecdote shows of how much less value land was in those days. However, she did recognise the rights of her neighbours to a share of the common, of which she occasionally took a large portion, by giving them a jolly feast at the Christmas season. It was really a good feast, tradition says, that they did not soon forget. There was a public-house at Hell Gill, called The Checkers,* kept by Jemmy Taylor. Also there was a beerhouse at Outh Gill, called The Gate. Quite modern. It was opened by Mr. John Dickinson. The name of the farm, which was The Gate, suggested the sign. Under the sign were the words:

> This gate hangs well and hinders none,
> Refresh and pay and travel on.

There are the following Latin words over a loft outer door at Outh Gill (the property of Captain Grimshaw) which has evidently belonged to an older building; most likely a public-house:

"Hospes inire jubet justos exire nefastos."

The landlord bids honest folk to enter, and knives to depart.

The old inn to which the Latin inscription originally belonged stood where the new barn opposite the Smithy at Outh Gill now

---

* A common sign of a public house. The arms, I understand, of the Arundels, who were the first to possess the exclusive right of selling foreign wines. This was in the reign of Edward IV.

stands. The old building, which had degenerated into a barn, was pulled down some thirty years ago. There are those who can remember some features, such as a brick oven, which testified to its former use as a dwelling house.

The present public-house was built by Mr. John Dickinson in the year 1870, when the licence was taken out. Its first landlord was Wm. Thompson. Its sign is The Castle Inn, so called, of course, after Pendragon Castle. A turnpike gate used to stand a short distance above this house.

There were occasional incursions of Scots through the dale on their way to the Craven district. Their course was by Soulby and Green Law. There is a tradition that in the year 1715, while the Scots were coming south to uphold the claims of the Pretender, "a merrie neet" was being held here; the news was announced, with the addition that they were marching towards Mallerstang. This had the effect of breaking up the party; the men hid their pewter and prepared for resistance.

Some time not long antecedent to 1695, several of the tenants of the Lord of the Manor enclosed common, in one case at Hanging Lunds, and in the other at Aisgarth *alias* Aisgill, without the consent of the Lord of the Manor. In the year 1695 they formally and by deed made their submission to the Lord of the Manor, each set of encroachers agreeing to pay the yearly rent of £4 to the Lord of the Manor, payable at Martinmas and Whitsuntide, to continue for 21 years, expiring 16th May, 1716. The following is a copy of the deed:

"We whose names are hereto subscribed customary tenants to the Rt. honble. Thos. Earl of Thanet Island &c. at Aisgarth alias Aisgill within the forest or dale of Mallerstang parish of the manor or lordship of Ky. Stephen in the county of Westmld. Having in the year of our Lord God one thousand six hundred and ninety four improved, inclosed, or walled in parcell of the common or waste ground at Hell gill woad near Hell gill bridge called Aisgarth alias Aisgill pasture within the said fforest or dale, and made the same a a pasture or grassing for cattle without the privity, license, or consent of the above said Earl whereby we are trespassers to the said Earl and have made ourselves subject to actions at law for the same.

"We do therefore hereby submit ourselves to the above said Earl and become farmers and lessors thereof, and do hereby jointly and severally covenant, promise and agree to, and write the above said Earl to pay unto the said Earl his heirs, executors and assigns the clear yearly rent of four pounds of lawfull money of England at the feast of St. Martin the Bishop in winter, and the feast of Pentecost yearly by equal portions for the same the first payment thereoff to commence at Martinmas next. In witness whereof we have hereto set our hands the sixteenth day of May in the seventh year of the reign of our Sovereign Lord William the third by the grace of God King of England, Scotland, France, and Ireland – Defender of the faith etc. and in the year of our Lord 1695.

"Signed and delivered on stamped parchment by Henry Bousfield, Henry Shaw, senior, Henry Whitfield, Robert Atkinson, Agnes Shaw for her son John, Richard Moreland for Ellen Shaw, and Wm. Whitfield in the presence of us—
Thomas Carleton.
Richard Waller.
William Binflosk
Thomas Longfellow*

Henry Bousfield.
John Shaw, snr.
Henry Whitfield.
Robert Atkinson.
Agnes Shaw on behalf of John Shaw her son, an infant } a.

Richard Moreland on behalf of Ellen Shaw his sister, being lame } I for R

Another submission of the tenants on the same date and under similar circumstances, owing to the taking in of Hanging Lunds, was

"Signed and delivered on stamped parchment by William Whitfield, Thomas Whitfield, senr., Thomas Whitfield, jun., William Kirkbride, and Wm. Kirkbride for his son Thomas, in the presence of us
Thomas Carleton
Richard Waller.
William Binflosk.
Thomas Longfellow.

Willyam Whitfield.
Thomas Whitfield, snr., II his mark
Thomas Whitfield, jun., T his mark
William Kirkbride, his X mark
William Kirkbride on the behalf of Thomas X Kirkbride, his son, his mark

Occasionally there were boundary riding disputes by the representatives of other manors. These frontier differences arose out of a difference of claim in some portion of the boundary. At the boundary riding, therefore, a representative of the lord of the adjoining manor, in consequence of a notice received from the agent of the other lord of the manor, appeared upon the scene at the appointed time, and uttered a decided protest when the boundary of the lord of the manor whom he represented was invaded and claimed by the neighbouring lord. Meanwhile, the

---

* The name Longfellow is by no means common; and its coincidence with the name of the great Americnn poet struck me. Through my friend, the Rev. J. Wharton, vicar of Stainnore, I learn that when the poet Longfellow was in the Lake District a few years ago, he said in the Assembly Room, Penrith, that he was a Cumberland man in two senses- i.e., Cumberland in the United States of America, and that his family originally came from Cumberland in England.

lord of the adjoining manor, or his agent, went over the disputed portion and included it in his boundary. At such points the protests were looked for. The present steward of Ravenstonedale, Mr. Anthony Metcalfe-Gibson, once told me that four generations of Anthony Metcalfes, beginning with his great grandfather, had been stewards, and had gone down to one of the disputed points of the Ravenstonedale boundary at Cautley at different times to make a protest, that the claim may not be ignored or lost. In 1710, when the representatives of the Right Honourable Thomas, Earl of Thanet, met the officers of Lord Wharton, who were riding the boundary of Swaledale, we read that they were correct, "save that in carrying their flag from the said High Seat to ye grey stone in Careless Bank the said Earl Wharton's officers surrounded about fifty acres of the said Earl of Thanet's waist ground belonging to his manor or dale of Mallerstang aforesaid as wee believe. And the said Mr. Carleton [Earl of Thanet's steward] then told the said Earl of Wharton's officers that in so carrying their flagg they carried it wrong, and that the several bounder marks above was the true known ancient bounder marks deviding the said Earl's said mannors and dales; and desired to see the said Earl Wharton's bounder roll, but they

did not produce or show any; only the said M. E. Smales showed a paper, in which some of the said bounder marks were named."

From the foregoing it would appear that the protests were not merely matter of course affairs, but that they were very distinctive and decided. I have also a record of "a stop made to Mr. Lowther's officers riding their pretended bounder of Ravenstonedale, adjoining to the Earl of Thanet's mannors of Kirkby Stephen and Mallerstang, 19th August, 1730. The boundary was ridden by Mr. Thomas Whelpdale and Mr. James Watson, stewards and agents for Robert Lowther, Esqre. They were opposed by Mr. Richard Strother, steward to the Earl of Thanet.

"And the said Richard Strother then told the said Mr. Whelpdale, and the company along with him, that the said Earl of Thanets bounder marks for the mannor of Kirkby Stephen went along from the said hurrock of stones, at the out edge of Ash Fell, down through tarn wett mire to tarn wet hole, thence to the highway leading from Kirkby Stephen to Sedbergh, thence along on that highway to Scandall bridge, otherwise Stanerskew bridge, thence up Scandall beck to the head thereof, up between the coal shafts by the side of Middletong to where Ky. Stephen bounder meets with Mallerstang, thence eastward to Wildbore fell pike, joining to Mallerstang bounder all the way, thence by the edge of Wildbore fell next Ravenstonedale to the hurrock of stones on Scandall head, thence as heaven water deals to bland stone, and thence to a hurrock of stones on Galloway Gates; and then told the said Mr. Whelpdale, and other company along with him, that they ought to ride by the bounder marks above mentioned, and discharged them from coming within the said early bounder marks, and told them that if they did they would be trespassers."

I have also a record of a "stop made to Mr. Lowther's officers riding their pretended bounder of Naitby, adjoining to the Earl of Thanet's mannor of Mallestang. Augt. 18th, 1730.".... And the said Richard Strother then read over unto the said Mr. Whelpdale, and other company there present, so much of the said Earl of Thanet's manor or Lordship of Mallerstang from the said Mr. Lowther's manor or Lordship of Naitby as follows, viz.: Beginning at Water gate scar, thence through Sopkeld, otherwise Killing close, to a place where a crab tree formerly stood, and was marked by Henry Lord Clifford, great grandfather to George Earl of

Cumberland, as his bounder, near which place, in the year of our Lord 1651, when these bounders were rid for the Right Honble. Anne, late Countess Dowager of Pembroke, stood an ash tree, which upon that occasion was marked A. P. as a bounder mark, Thence through Ashbank (which is also part of Sopkeld) where an house formerly was built, through which house the bounder went, thence to the foot of Naitgill by Ravenscar to Kitchingill foot, thence up Kitchingill to Tailbrigg Sike, thence up Tailbrigg sike to the row of coves, thence to the gingling cove, thence through Lampes moss to a greystone in Careless Bank on the north east of the fell end. And the said Richard Strother then told the said Mr. Whelpdale that they ought to ride the bounder of Nateby by these bounder marks. But the said Mr. Whelpdale told the said Richard Strother that the bounder marks of their bounder of Naitby were as follows, and that they would ride that way, viz.: From Watergate Scarr up the river Eden to Blewgrass, thence along Eden to Agill Sike foot, so up Agill sike to Stoney gate that rises on to the fells end, then over the height of ffells end down in a direct line to Greystone. And the said Mr. Whelpdale said they claimed all the royalties within their said pretended bounder for Mr. Lowther; but one Mathew Robinson one of the said Mr. Lowther's tenants of Naitby said that when he rode the said bounder of Naitby with the late Lord Wharton's officers they did not then claim the royalties of a place they included within their pretended bounder called the Bells, but only a right of common and turbary. Notwithstanding which the said Mr. Whelpdale and those along with him rode their bounder of Naitby, by the pretended bounders of Naitby in the manner they did have included above three hundred acres of the said Earl's liberties – common or wast ground belonging to the said manor or lordship of Mallerstang, all which we shall be ready to prove when thereunto required. Witness our hands this eighteenth day of August, Anno Dni. 1730.

Tenants of Mallerstang	Joseph Shaw. Thomas Ward.	Richard Strother Thos. Busey Chr. Harrison, Joseph Thompson, Thos. Yeatts, John Barnett, Charles Hastwell, Miles Hutchinson, Jos. Thornton,

(Richard Strother, Thos. Busey, Chr. Harrison — Persons not interested; Joseph Thompson, Thos. Yeatts, John Barnett — not interested; Charles Hastwell, Miles Hutchinson, Jos. Thornton — Persons interested.)

The most recent dispute grew out of the construction of the Midland Railway. In the year 1869, the Midland Railway Company, pursuant to an Act of Parliament, gave notice to the landowners of Mallerstang that they would take possession of several plots of land, some of it being in dispute. A meeting was held of the Commoners at Kirkby Stephen, 11th January, 1870. The first point in the dispute was the extent of Birket, and the second the rights over it. During the trial the former claim was relinquished.

The nature of the claim on the part of Lord Lonsdale was that a deed was executed in 1590, whereby the Earl of Cumberland granted to his predecessor in estate [Lord Wharton and his tenants] the *exclusive* right of pasturage; the landowners of Mallerstang contending, on the other hand, that the landholders of Wharton had a right with them to the herbage, but not an exclusive right, and it was decided in their favour.

The value of the common land of Mallerstang, disputed and undisputed, was paid over to the Committee appointed by the

Commoners of Mallerstang. The question of costs has not yet been finally settled.

The boundary ridings are observed at varying intervals of time, not often exceeding that of a generation. The circumstances of these ridings are often those of excitement to the male portion of the community, the conspicuous figure being at such times the bearer of the flag, accompanied by a representative of the lord of the manor, if not the lord of the manor himself, and many of the leading men in the parish. The last boundary riding of Mallerstang took place on the 12th day of July, 1865, when Mr. Parkin Blades, and others, carried the colours. I understand that Miss Maria Atkinson, of Dale foot, rode horseback with the party, being the first lady that had accompanied a boundary riding party since Lady Anne of Pembroke, in the year 1651, when tradition says she not only rode the boundary, but cut A. P. in an ash tree which was a boundary mark.

The representative of the lord of the manor at the last boundary riding was Edward Heelis, Esqre. The legal document marked "G," which, through the kindness of the aforesaid Mr. Heelis I can furnish you a copy of, is as follows:

"The boundary of the manor or lordship of Mallerstang, ridden and perambulated for Sir Richard Tufton, Baronet, lord of the said manor or lordship, on Wednesday, the twelfth day of July, in the twenty-ninth year of the reign of our Sovereign Lady Victoria, by the grace of God of the United Kingdom of Great Britain and Ireland Queen, Defender of the Faith, and in the year of our Lord one thousand eight hundred and sixty-five.

1. Beginning at Watergate Scar.

2. Thence through Sopkeld otherwise Killing Close to a place where a crab tree formerly stood which was marked by Henry Lord Clifford, great grandfather to George, late Earl of

Cumberland, as his boundary mark; near which place in the year of our Lord one thousand six hundred and fifty-one, when the said boundary was ridden for the Right Honourable Ann, Countess Dowager of Pembroke stood an ash tree which upon that occasion was marked A. P. as a boundary mark.

3. Thence through Ash Bank [which is also part of Sopkeld] where a house formerly was built through which house the boundary went.

4. Thence to the foot of Naitgill.

5. Thence up Naitgill by Ravenscar to Kitchin Gill foot.

6. Thence up Kitchen Gill to Taillbridge Syke.

7. Thence up Taillbridge Syke to the row of coves.

8. Thence to the Gingling Cove.

9. Thence through Lamps Moss to a grey stone in Careless Bank, on the north east of Fells End.

10. Thence to the lower end of Seavyman in Ulgill head.

11. Thence to the north end of High seat.

12. Thence as Heaven water deals to the south end of High seat.

13. Thence over Little Sleddle head to Gregory Chapel.

14. Thence along Gregory Band to a hurrock of stones at Langill Head.

15. Thence to the height of Hugh Seat Morville.

16. —Thence as Heaven water deals to the Skaith of Skaites. From thence the boundary used to go to Capel Mey Skyke, thence down Capel May Syke to Withow Syke, and thence to White Birk but disputes having arisen touching the boundaries between the Earl of Thanet and the township and manor of High Abbotside and the township of Lower Abbotside and manor of Dale Grange otherwise Lower Abbotside in the parish of Aisgarth in the county of York or one of them, the Commissioners appointed under the Act of Parliament of the fifth year of the reign of His late Majesty

King George the Fourth for inclosing lands within the said manors did by their award dated the fifteenth day of September 1827 fix and determine the same as follows:

The following is a full record of the decision of Commissioners referred to in Boundary Ridings, 1840 and 1865, at No.16:

"Abbotside Commons.

"Whereas an act of Parliament was made and passed in the fifth year of the reign of his present Majesty King George the Fourth intituled – 'An act for inclosing lands in the Township and manor of High Abbotside and in the township of Lower Abbotside and manor of Dale Grange, otherwise Lower Abbotside in the parish of Aisgarth in the county of York.' And whereas considerable doubts have arisen and existed touching and concerning the boundary between the said manors of one of them and the manor of Mallerstang in the parish of Kirkby Stephen in the co. of Westmorland.

"Now we Jeremiah Coulton and Thomas Bradley the Commissioners named and appointed in and by the said act having given due notice of our intention to ascertain, set out, fix and determine, the said boundary to the several persons interested therein in the manner required by law and having met pursuant to such notice at the house of Mr. Robert Brunskill the Bull Inn at Shaw Parrock in Lunds in the parish of Aisgarth aforesaid on Monday the twenty seventh day of August last, and on several subsequent days and times by virtue of several adjournments of our said meeting, and having heard the several parties interested therein or their agents or solicitors, and having examined various witnesses upon oath touching and concerning the said boundary, and having viewed and inspected the same as claimed by the Lords of the said manors respectively, and the owners of lands and tenements within the same, have ascertained and set out, and do fix and determine the same to commence and begin at a place called White Birks, and to proceed from thence direct to the water of Hell Gill, and so up the said water to the first sike (on the east side thereof) above Lamb Folds, and from thence in a direct line as the same is now staked out to the Skarth of Skaiths and from thence in a direct line as the same is staked out to the boundary of the manor of Muker in the parish of Grinton, in the said county of York which said boundary is particularly described and delineated in the map or plan thereof hereunto annexed.

"Dated the fifteenth day of September one thousand eight hundred and twenty seven.

"JERE. COULTON.
"THOMAS BRADLEY."

17. From the said Skaith of Skaites in a direct line to the first Syke (on the east side thereof) above Lamb Folds.

18. Thence down Hell Gill water to the White Birks where the dispute ended.

19. Thence up Stubbing Rigg to Middle Gill, otherwise Smithy Gill Howe.

20. Thence to a hurrock of stones at the east end of Swarth Fell, called Swarth Fell pike.

21. Thence to a hurrock of stones in Galloway Gates.

22. Thence as Heaven water deals to Blandston.

23. Thence to a hurrock of stones on Scandall Head.

24. Thence to the pike on Wildbore Fell.

25. Thence to the top of Mickle Arke.

26. Then ce along Stoney Gate to Merepott.

27. Thence to the great cove on Greenlaw Head.

28. Thence to the head of Fothergill Beck.

29. Thence down Fothergill Beck to Eden Water.

30. Thence up Eden Water to Water Gate Scar.

This boundary was ridden and perambulated in the presence of us.

Signed—

Edwd. Heelis, junr	John Dickinson.
George Blades.	Alex. Hogg.
Wm. S. Fulton.	Thos. Mitchell.
G. H. Bailey.	Mark Ellwood.
W. Wilson.	John Metcalf.
J. Grimshaw.	Edwd. Forsyth.
Robert Medcalfe.	John Morland, jnr.
John H. Scott.	Frances Maria Atkinson.
James Allan.	Joseph Barker Hind.
Thos. Atkinson.	James his ✘ mark Graham.
Robt. Atkinson.	Michl. Morland.
Wm. Richardson.	Anthony Allen.
John Richardson.	William his ✘ mark Mounsey.
oseph Metcalfe.	John Dalton
James Ellwood.	Richard his ✘ mark Dent.
Joseph Ellinson.	Wm. Fothergill.
Matthew his ✘ mark Metcalfe.	James Wright.
Stephen Atkinson.	—
Wm. Allen.	
John Richardson.	Flag Bearers
Matthew Metcalfe.	Parkin Blades.
John his ✘ mark Atkinson.	George Currah.
William Harper.	John Richardson.
Parkin Blades.	Joseph Parker Hind.
Wm. Balden.	—
John Richardson, junr.	John Richardson.
Matthew Muckelt, yeoman.	Wm. Wilson.
George Currah	Matthew Metcalfe.

Mallerstang Boundary.

Notice is hereby given that the boundary of the Manor or Lordship of Mallerstang in the County of Westmorland will be ridden and perambulated by the Agents and Tenants of Sir Richard Tufton Baronet, Lord of the said manor, or Lordship on Wednesday the twelfth day of July next and that they will commence the said riding and perambulation at a place called Watergate Scarr by nine o'Clock in the forenoon of the said day when and where all Lords of the several adjoining manors or Lordships and all other persons concerned may attend if they think proper.

Given under my hand this twenty first day of June 1865.

JOHN HEELIS
Steward of the said manor or Lordship.

Copies of the above notice were inserted in the *Kendal Mercury* of the twenty fourth of June and the first and eighth of July 1865 and in the *Cumberland ancl Westmoreland Advertiser* of the twenty seventh of June and the fourth day of July 1865.

I hereby certify that a true copy of the above notice was affixed by me on the door of the parish Church of Kirkby Stephen and on the door of the chapel of Mallerstang the twenty seventh day of June 1865.

PARKIN BLADES.

Mallerstang Boundary.

I do hereby give you notice that the boundary of the Manor or Lordship of Mallerstang in the County of West morland will be ridden and perambulated by the Agents and Tenants of Sir Richard Tufton Baronet, Lord of the said Manor or Lordship on

Wednesday the 12th day of July next, and that they will commence the said riding and perambulation at a place called Watergate Scarr by nine o'clock in the forenoon of the said day, when and where you may attend if you think proper.

Given under my hand this twenty-first day of June 1865.
JOHN HEELIS
Steward of the said manor or Lordship.

Copies of the above notice were delivered as follows: To the Reverend John Winn one of the Lords of the manor of Griesdale and to Henry Thompson Esqre. Lord of the manor of Uldale on the seventh day of July 1865; and to Thomas Cleasby and Matthew Thompson Esqres. Lords of the manor of White Birch and to Matthew Thompson Esqre. another of the Lords of the manor of Grisedale on the tenth day of July 1865.

PARKIN BLADES
Bailiff of the said Manor or Lordship.

The perambulation commenced at about nine o'clock in the morning, and ended at about four in the afternoon. All dined in the open air at Watergate Bottom, and the company partook of as much food and drink as they liked at the expense of the lord of the manor. Such occasions are purposely characterised by a great deal of jollity, such as wrestling and racing, &c., that they may be well remembered by the young folks of the party.

The river will next claim our attention. The name given to it by the Romans was *Ituna*. Its present name, as you know full well, is Eden. The derivation of the word Eden is a matter of some uncertainty. According to one derivation, it means, as a compound, water and dale, *i.e.,* water of the dales or valleys – *ea,* water; and *den,* a deep wooded valley (Anglo-Saxon); (2)

according to others, *don* (Celtic), water or river, and an unexplained prefix; (3) Phillips (" Rivers and Mountains of Yorkshire," page 199) adopts the derivation *Ed-dain* (Celtic), the gliding stream. In this inquiry, however, we must bear in mind that we are analysing the word Eden rather than ascertaining the cause why your river was called by that name. And in studying this question the obvious inquiry forces itself upon the mind whether it has not a distinct relation to the Eden of the Bible, of which the previous etymology holds good, and of which we read: "And a river went out of Eden to water the garden: and from thence it was parted and became into four heads." When, therefore, your "rude fathers" gave the name Eden to the river which includes also the valley; whether they were Ancient Britons (for the light of God's truth was here before the Saxons came), or whether they were Saxons, my opinion is that they were acquainted with the Eden of Scripture, and that, struck with the beauty of the valley, they called it Eden; and, without flattering you or those living lower down the dale, I do not hesitate to say that the vale of the Eden is, in the summer season, paradisaical in its beauty. The Rev. J. Wharton, Vicar of Stainmore, in one of the notes which he has kindly furnished me with on local names, says: "The word Eden contains a root signifying water, and there are four streams of this name in the island." The Eden takes its rise in Mallerstang at Blackfell moss, close to the boundary of Yorkshire. Four years ago I traced it to its source, in company with Mr. Atkinson Metcalfe-Gibson. We commenced from Hell Gill Bridge, and a quarter of a mile above it struck down into the bed of the stream, and continued in it more or less until we came to a point where two streams meet. We followed the one on the left hand until it was lost among runnels in the ling. The source of the other branch is, I understand, similar. Hence the source of the river is called "Eden Springs." On what a lofty height it takes its rise, and how wild and grand! Camden says, in speaking of this very spot: "Such a dreary waste and horrid silent wilderness that certain rivulets that creep here are called Hell-becks, rivers of hell. In this part the goats, deer, and stags of extraordinary size with branching horns find a secure retreat." On that same range two other rivers rise on the other side of the watershed. They are the Ure and the Swale. The Eden runs north and falls into the Solway Firth. The other two proceed in an easterly direction and find their way to the German Ocean.

The principal small affluents of the Eden in Mallerstang are rivulets in Stone-close Gill, Aisgill, Deep Gill, and Thrang Beck. In the year 1850, Mr. William Mounsey – relatives of whom still reside at Carlisle and are respected there – after he had travelled in Egypt and other Eastern lands, determined to trace his native river to its source. This he did, and to commemorate this pilgrimage, had the following inscription engraved upon a stone – Dent marble -and set up at, or, more correctly speaking, near, the source of the river. The inscription, with its Christian symbols,* is as follows:

Copy Of Inscription Near The Source Of The Eden.

Φευγωμεν συν νηυσι φιλην 'ες πατριδα γαιαν

Διξεο ψυχης 'οχετον οθεν η τινι ταξει
Σωματι θητευσας επι ταξιν αφ' 'ης ερρυης
Αυθις αναστησεις ιερψλογψεργον ενωσας

Πατρις δε ημιν οθεν παρηλθομεν και πατηρ εκει

Itinere apud ostium suscepto fonte tenus confecto
Genio Iturnae et nymphis V. S. YESNUOM SUMLEILUG
Eremita peregrinans XV. Martii A.C. MDCCCL.

—

Translation.

"Let us flee with our ships to our dear native land."
Homer. "Iliad," II., 140.

"Seek the channel of the soul – whence, or by what means, after being the slave of the body, thou shalt raise it [the soul] again to the position from which thou wert derived, uniting thy deed to the holy Word."
 [The Greek is quoted by Coleridge – "Friend," Vol. III., p. 82 – from "Zoroastr. Oracula, Initio. Edit. Opsopoei. 1599."]

"We have a country from which we came and our father is there."
 [I do not know the source of this quotation.]

"Having commenced his journey at the mouth and finished it at the source, William Mounsey, a wandering hermit fulfilled his vow to the Genius and nymphs of the Eden on the 15th of March in the year of Christ 1850."

---

*They are, I presume, the symbol of the Trinity, and the Tau (T) Cross of our Saviour inverted.

Mallerstang – Arable land.................3 acres, 2 roods, 34 perches.
            Meadow......................851 acres, 1 rood, 19 perches.
            Pasture........................1053 acres, 5 perches.
            Common....................3000 acres.
            Road and River ....36 acres, 2 roods, 24 perches.

            Total............................4944 acres, 2 roods, 24 perches.

Of late the land has been much improved by draining, and now there is no arable land; and it appears from the Tithe Award that there never has been much, as there is no rectorial or corn tithe award; it is all either meadow or pasture.

In the foregoing the Common is estimated at 3,000 acres,

which must have been a guess, as it had not been measured. The following are the various particulars of the dimensions of the common, river, public roads, and land planted, as given in the Ordnance map, and in the schedule thereto headed "No. on plan," "Area in acres," and "Remarks":

MALLERSTANG

No. on Plan	Remarks.	Area in Acres.
1.	Moor	463·669
2.	Public road	2·585
3.	River, &c	11·773
4.	Waste	1.057
5.	Stream	234
14.	Plantation	175
26.	Wood, &c	3.526
53.	"	1.261
56.	" part of	1.393
72		2.283
85A.	Public road	955
86.	Pasture, &c. (encroachment, and now common or waste again	611

96.	Public road	831
104.	Castle ruin.	2.494
127.	Underwood	582
142.	Occupation road (Castlethwaite)	1.016
191.	Public road	15.287
194.	Waste, &c	776
198.	Pinfold	014
208.	Stream	055
215.	Plantation	042
247.	"	118
263.	River, &c	16.880
272.	Wood	377
375.	Plantation	118
431.	Wood, &c	117
432.	Plantation	912
436.	Stream	374
438.	River, &c	3.275
440.	Wood, &c	189
468.	"	959
487.	Plantation	210
488.	Public road	070
493.	Wood, &c	199
495.	Moor (west of Eden)	2274.055
496.	Public road	2.151
498.	Moor (east of Eden)	3613.976
499.	Public road	4.872
502.	" "	463

Summary.

			Acres.	Acres.
1.	Moor		463.669	
4.	Actually moor		1.057	
86.	"	"	611	
142.	"	" (occupation road)	1.016	
194.	Waste		776	
495.	Moor		2274.055	
498.	"		3613.976	

Total of common, exclusive of public roads and river   6355.160
Inclosed land, exclusive of public roads and river.   1965.383

Public roads, viz.:

2.	....	2.585
85A	....	955
96	....	831
191	....	15.287
488	....	070
496	....	2.151
499	....	4.872
502	....	463

	Total of public roads		27.214
3.	River	11.773	
5.	Practically part of river.......................	234	
263.	River	16.880	
438.	"	3.275	32.162

Total according to Ordnance Survey	8379.919

There is a sandstone quarry in the dale, situated at Swarthfell. It is not much worked at present, but it has furnished a great deal of stone for the roofing of houses in this and the adjoining parish of Ravenstonedale. A few years ago, a coal mine, on the common, reached by a road from Outhgill, was worked, and the coal was used by the inhabitants of this dale; but it never yielded much, and remained for some time unused. Now I understand that it is being worked again.

There is a lead mine at the Bells, at the foot of the dale, that was worked by the Peases, of Darlington, at first without success; whereupon the company offered a reward to any of the men who might discover a vein or pocket of lead, and the following is the late Mr. G. Blades' account of the result: "Jno. Scott of Southwaite got up early one morning with the hope and determination to discover a pocket in a particular part of the shaft where he expected to find it. He attacked the spot in question with his pick, and soon found to his satisfaction that he had discovered a pocket.

Having convinced himself of his success, he sat down and smoked his pipe; happy no doubt as a king. The discovery was made known to the Peases. They worked it very successfully. The lead was found in a very pure state, and some of the lumps were so large that it took two or three men to turn them over, and when they were split open they shone like silver. One piece was sent to Appleby Castle as a specimen of what the mine produced. The general opinion is that the Pease Co. for many years worked with much profit this now disused mine." Mines of copper and tin have also been worked here, the former at Aisgill moor, where there are, or were lately, the remains of a "smelt mill." The tin mine was worked in Anger holme woad, by persons of the name of Shaw. But neither the copper nor tin mines seem to have been worked with any profit, most probably owing to the cost of carriage and the want of coal. The refuse stones from the tin mines, being of a whitish substance, were sold for stoning hearth stones, by a well-known character in his day, and to whom I shall have occasion to refer again later on, known by the name of "Joss Dick or Mauston Dick."

But it is quite time that I called your attention to the people – those that are still remembered for their character or social position – and also to the manners and customs of the people generally, and the first and most remarkable personage is Captain Atkinson. He was captain of the militia, and was a man of considerable social influence. He owned, I am told, the following estates – Dale Foot, New Hall, Mill Becks, Winton (occupation of George Winter), and Wharton. He seems to have been a zealous supporter of the rule of Oliver Cromwell, and as evidence of it, we are informed "that when Captain Atkinson, a native of Winton (and hanged with two others, April 1, 1664, for being concerned in Kaber plot), attempted to choose a roundhead mayor by force of arms, the town (Appleby) resisted, and chose a moderate man; and though this man, Captain Atkinson, induced the Protector to impose a new charter upon them, yet they kept their old one to the last." At the Restoration Captain Atkinson adhered to the laws which the nation generally had set aside; and gathering a band of followers together, rose in rebellion against the constituted authority at Kaber Rigg. He and his men seem to have offered very small resistance ere he was taken prisoner, and subsequently tried by a special commission as a traitor. In this trial it is said that Lady Pembroke was deeply interested, and had set her mind on his execution. He was hanged within the grounds of Appleby Castle, in the year 1664. The following remarkable tradition was told me by Mr. G. Blades, and was confirmed by some of Captain Atkinson's descendants:

On the morning of the execution, a king's officer arrived at Stainmore, and asked at the inn whether there was any particular news. Whereupon they informed him that Captain Atkinson had been executed that morning. "why," he replied, "I have his reprieve in my pocket." His property was hence forth confiscated; and his eldest son, who was unmarried, lived with the Earl of Thanet. His widow and the rest of his children lived at Dale Foot, where the rent paid for a number of years afterwards was nominal, and where his descendants continue to this day; thus reminding us that we see displacement from violent causes of social as well as geological strata.

On the other side of the valley, and within sight of Dale Foot, is the seat of the Wharton family; and it is very well known that Philip, Lord Wharton, who was a contemporary of Captain Atkinson, was as decided a Parliamentarian as he was. His estates, too, in the course of three subsequent generations, were confiscated in the reign of Queen Anne. The descendants of that family, too, are amongst us; and men who bear the name of Wharton, and inherit the traditions and blue blood of the race, are to be found not only amongst the middle class, but amongst the noble army of workers whose arms would be the plough or the scythe, and whoso motto is, "Industry must prosper." When we look at these ups and downs, to be found more or less in every district, we are led to attach increasingly less importance to the accident of birth and station, and more to character; most heartily singing with the Poet Laureate:

> "Kind hearts are more than coronets,
> And simple faith than Norman blood."

Of those who have gone out of this dale and risen in the world, you have only one conspicuous example, and he was John Blades. He lived at Lunds, which is a little beyond your township; still, his kinsfolk lived here, so that I think you may claim him. He went up to London about ninety years ago, and through Mr. William Milner, of Tottenham Court Road, I learn that it is current at the Guildhall that he went to London with the proverbial halfcrown only in his pocket; and it is believed that when, on his first arrival, he was walking down Ludgate Hill, he asked some one at the door of the house of which he afterwards became sole proprietor, for a situation, he was at once engaged as a porter. Evidently he attended well to his humble duties, and by so doing was advanced to something better. The late Mr. Blades told me that he was for some time a commercial traveller of the house, and represented them not only in England but on the Continent as well, where he solicited orders for cut and ornamental glass of the most sumptuous description. The next step in his advancement was his marriage with his employer's only daughter and child. Owing to this largely, be succeeded to the business; and from the position he afterwards came to occupy in the City of London, he must have been greatly respected there. Mr. G. Blades had the impression that he became Lord Mayor of London, but through the careful investigation of Mr. Milner, who is himself related to the same family, I learn that he became one of the Sheriffs of London and Middlesex. He was a liberal benefactor of the City Guild to which he belonged – "The Glass-sellers' Company"- and he is said to have made, at his own cost, the opening from Fleet Street to St. Bride's Church, which brought the latter into view.*

You may be interested to know that the office of Sheriffs of the City of London and Sheriff of Middlesex is held jointly by two persons who are nominated by the Lord Mayor and elected by the Livery of the City. The Livery are the freemen of the City who have taken upon them the livery and clothing and become members of one of the City Guilds, which position also gives a vote for members of Parliament for the City.

The sheriffs are elected for one year. They do not always become or seek to become Lord Mayors, their office being quite independent, although much associated with that of the Lord

---

*Since writing the above I have received, through the kindness of Mr. Wm. Milner, the following note from.Mr. G. T. T. Plowman, one of the churchwardens at present of St. Bride's. He says; "He [Mr. Blades] entered the parish of St. Bride in 1779, was Constable in 1787, and Churchwarden in 1812. He erected a tablet in the vestibule of the church as an affectionate tribute to the memory of his three brothers. As regards the approach to the church from Fleet Street, there is an engraving in the vestry showing the improvement, and bearing the names of 21 gentlemen with Mr. Blades as treasurer, and stating that the improvement was made by public subscription at a cost of £10,000." It would appear that the alteration was effected by a public subscription, but as Mr. Blades was the treasurer, he was most likely a liberal contributor to that work.

Mayor. On the other hand, the Lord Mayor, who is elected from amongst the Aldermen, must have been Sheriff before he can become Lord Mayor.

The office of Sheriff is analogous with that of the High Sheriff of a County; but the Sheriffs of London, from their connection with the Lord Mayor, have to appear with him upon many ceremonial occasions, and they share with him the cost of the Lord Mayor's banquet and procession.

The office of Sheriff is also sometimes held by men of somewhat higher social and commercial position than those who now become Lord Mayors. The Lord Mayor, although almost always moderately rich and of respectable position, has never, at any rate for many years, been one of the leading bankers or merchants of the City, but generally a prosperous tradesman. The Sheriffs have occasionally been of higher standing.

Mr. Blades held the office of Sheriff of London in the year 1813, when another North of England man, M·. George Scholey, of Sandal, in Yorkshire, was Lord Mayor. Mr. G. Blades, in his communication to me, remarked – "Mr. Blades came down from London to see us all, I should think, about sixty years ago. I, with others, dined with him at Hawes. I should have known him to be a Blades, for he had a nice red cheek." His father's name was Thomas Blades, who was a statesman in the possession of a farm at West End.

Of such a career you may be proud, and it should act as a splendid stimulus to the young men of the district. At the same time do not fail to appreciate the industry and manly integrity which one is bound to recognise as features which belong not only to this dale but to this county; and remember that a field receives its colour not from a brilliant flower here and there, but from the prevailing hue of the flowers which grow upon it. In other words, whilst you may be proud of one who rose to a high social position, it is of far more importance that you should keep manifest the evidence that you are, as I believe you to be, honest, industrious, and true.

LECTURE IV.

MALLERSTANG is in no way remarkable for its archaeological remains, apart from its castle. Still, there are some features of interest in it in this respect. In a paper read by Canon Greenwell, at Penrith, at the first meeting of the Antiquarian and Archaeological Society, 1866, I find the following:

"On May 3lst we [Canon Simpson and himself] examined two cairns situated in Mallerstang on a piece of haugh land, just above the river Eden. The position of the cairns is unusual, as it is very uncommon to find them placed on low-lying ground. It has been sixty feet in diameter. We made a partial examination, but did not find the interment; several clippings of flint and numerous pieces of charcoal testified to the sepulchral character of the mound, and Mr. Simpson and I propose to complete the investigation on some future occasion.* About fifty yards from this was a smaller cairn, fifteen feet diameter, and one and a half feet high. In the centre of this, in a hollow, sunk in the surface of the ground, one and a quarter feet deep, *was the deposit of the burnt bones of a body* under a flat stone. Above them, on the north side, were the remains of a small urn of the type called "an incense cup," much

---

*Canon Simpson tells me that no further discoveries have been made.

decayed. It has been three inches high and three inches wide, and has one hole now, and probably had once two, through the side. This class of urn, the use of which is very difficult to understand, is by no means an unfrequent accompaniment of a burnt body. They are usually pierced with two holes, sometimes at the top, but as often near the bottom of the urn. They also occur without any holes, and sometimes with a large number through the side. I have one from Yorkshire which has twenty-seven holes in rows of three running round the urn. The whole surface of the urn from Mallerstang, even to the bottom, is covered with an ornamental pattern, made by punctures of a small pointed implement. In this cairn we found no flint.

We at the same time opened one of those rectangular mounds, called giants' graves, so many of which remain in the district, and which look like barrows, though of a rather uncommon shape. Several have been examined at various places, all of which showed no signs whatever of their being places of burial. They are certainly artificial, but I can offer no conjecture as to their origin or purpose."

Canon Simpson is of opinion that they are bracken stack bottoms, as they are generally found near a place where that plant seems to have abounded. They are found on the side of Smardale Gill, and in Ravenstonedale. When examined they have yielded no results. No doubt there is great probability in this conjecture; others incline to the opinion that in times remote, so remote perhaps as to be, properly speaking, pre-historic, the giants' graves, as they have for ages been called, were burial places.

Captain Grimshaw has in his possession an interesting document which furnishes a list of "those persons that is at full age within ye fforest of Mallerstange which is lyable to pay ye powle." It is without date, but Captain Grimshaw is of opinion that it is about 180 years old; and I should think that he is correct. It is uncertain what the object of the poll tax was, possibly to raise money towards a national subsidy, or towards defraying the expense of a levy of soldiers; for Nicholson and Burn say, "It is a vulgar mistake that this county paid no subsidies during the existence of the *border service,* as supposing it to be exempted from such payments merely upon that account." The list is as follows:

(First page.)	£	s.
"Widdow Atkinson, and one servant, wages £3, & 3 children ..		8
Edward ffothergill his wife & 2 children at age............................		4
Michaell ffothergill his wife & 3 children......................................		5
Thos. Knewstupp his wife & 2 children		4
Richard Hesleton & his wife		2
Jefrey Guy & his wife 2 ch		4
John ffothergill & his wife & 3 children..		5
Daniel Whitfield & his wife and one maidservant		3
Robert Guy and his wife..		2
George Harrison		1
Widdow Harrison one child		2
Thomas Whitfield & his wife..		2
Barthollomew Wharton & his wife and his mother		3
Robert Branthwaite Gent his wife .... and 2 servants, one wages 20s	5	2
		3
William Shaw & his wife		2
John Atkinson & his wife .... and one maid servant wages 20s.		4
		2
Widdow Shaw 1 child...		2
Henry Shaw and his wife .... and one maid servant wages 20s.		2
		2
Row: Wright		1
Widdow Loadman & 2 children...		3
Tho: Ward & his wife & 3 child		5

(Second page.) £ s.

	£	s.
Henry Whitfield & his wife		2
Tho. Dent Senior and his wife		2
Tho. Dent Junior and his wife		2
Michaell Wharton & his wife & child		3
John Wharton & his wife & 2 children		4
Jonathan Glidall and his wife }		2
and one maid servant		1
John Knewstupp & his mother		2
Widdow Turner & her daughter		2
Thos. Wright and one maid servant		2
Anthon Bell		1
Ralph Shaw & his sister & }		2
servant		1
John Atkinson		1
Tho: Knewstupp & his wife }		3
one maid seruant		1
Phillip Wharton & his wife		2
One maid sarvuant wagis 20s		2
Tho: ffothergill & his wife & one child }		3
2 chd		4
Willm Birkbeck his wife & mother }		
and his maid seruant wages 20s		2
Tho: Wharton & his wife		2
John Knewstupp his sister & servt		3
Jeferay fothergill		1
Widdow Hugginson 1 child		2
Briham Hugginson & his wife }		2
and seraunt		1
Willm Bulmar & his wife		2
Tho: Shaw & his wife 1 child		3
John Hugginson & his wife 2 child:		4
Tho: Tunstall & his wife 3 child }		5
And one maid seruant wages 20s		2

(Third page.) £ s.

	£	s.
William Shaw and his wife one child }		4
and one maid seruant		
Widdow Birkdaile & her daughter		2

Cudbart Shaw & his wife 1 child	3
Adam Shaw & his mother	2
Robert Shaw & his wife 1 man	3
one maid seruant wages 20s	2
Henry Shaw & his wife 2 child	4
Tho: Blades & his wife 2 child	4
Matthew Whitefield & his wife	2
One maid seruant	1
Henry 'Whitfield & his wife 3 child	5
and Isabea Robinson	1
Tho Whitfield & his wife & sister 2 child	5
Widdow shaw & her sonn & daughter	3
Henry Shaw & his wife	2
John Knewstuppe 2 children	3
Rowland ffothergill & his wife & cousin	3
Widdow Turner	2
Tho: Thorneborow & his wife	3
and one maid seruant	1
John Shaw & his mother 2 child	4
Hugh Shaw & his wife 1 child	3
Tho: Shaw	1
Richard Tunstall & his wife 3 child	5
Richard Shaw & his wife one child	3
Willm Shaw his wife 1 child	
one maid servant	4
Widdow Dinsdall	1

Indorsement.
John Wharton
William Shaw is Apointed collector
hereof by the Commissionrs."

The number assessed I make to be 205, and reckoning 50 for such as were under the age of 15, make 255. In looking at these numbers we must remember that there were in early days houses so insignificant, shielings, one might call them, that they were passed over in any legal documents. The folks who lived in these primitive houses had only a field and small garth or pasture, called grassam, attached; indeed, the large pastures of to-day are divided into grassams. Their cows were turned out on the common during the day and came home for the night. The following are the more recent returns of the number of the population and of the houses:

	Houses.	Inhabitants.
In 1801	67	314
In 1813	53	249
In 1821		243
In 1831		256
In 1871, during the construction of the Midland Railway,		583
In 1881	60	271

Judging from the preceding figures there has been a diminution of the population since 1801, but it has not been very considerable. Nevertheless, it is the opinion of the aged and intelligent people with whom I have conversed that, taking into account the remains of foundations which they have discovered, and the houses they know of which have gone down, there must have been a considerably larger population 150 years ago than at present. I am told that at Sand Pot, and at Elm Gill, and at Aisgill, within recent memory there were clusters of houses, where now there are only two or three in each place, and there are traces of others farther back. Mr. G. Blades told me that in Sweet Close there was found a hearthstone with peat ashes upon it, and also, above Angerholme, a stone and ashes. At another place, not far away, stones were being dug out for a fence, and they came upon another hearthstone with peat ashes; and the ground work stone, shewed that it was a small house. Very much of the wood has disappeared. At one time it must have been considerable, for not only are roots constantly being turned up, but the names of divisions of the dale, such as Southwaite and Castlethwaite, and Hanging Lund bear evidence of considerable wood, and in addition to this many of the farms are called after trees, such as

> Birk-Birch-rigg
> Elm Gill
> Hazel Gill
> Sycamores.

The following are the names of fields:

> Ash bank
> Ellers-Alders
> Rowantree dale
> Hollin (holly) close
> Asps.

Of names of places you have Ash Bank, and White Birks Hill, and Birkett.

In the course of time much of the wood has been cut down, without being replaced by young trees. This process is apt to go on here and elsewhere, and so, in the course of time, a wooded district, such as yours has been, comes to be in no way remarkable for its abundance of trees. There is one handsome tree still standing on the land of Mr. Geo. Blades, and which he kindly took me to see. It is a sycamore, and is the handsomest tree of its kind I know of in the district.

In those days when the population was larger, and your fathers were more overshadowed with trees than you are now, the habits of the people, from all I can learn, were simpler. Knitting was a universal occupation, both for the men and women; indeed, it used to be said, when two young folks were "wed," that if they were good knitters they would do. The kind of knitting was the making of pop jackets and caps, such as those worn by sailors. They often spent an evening in each others houses, and this was called "going a sitting." They sat in a semicircle on stools, around the fire, and did their knitting exclusively by its light. At supper time bread and milk and cheese were brought out and put upon a "coppy" stool. Men as well as women engaged in knitting, with which they occupied themselves as they were walking along the road, or in interval when they were shepherding. Their work when done they took to James Law, of Outhgill, forty years ago. He kept a draper and grocer's shop, and the folks arranged to "wear" their earnings with him. He took the knitted work to Kendal, or sent it by the carrier. In the spring, his wife, Mary, a woman of some character, made a special journey to Kendal, and brought back gown pieces, from which the women of the dale made a selection, and the inspection of the aforesaid gown pieces on the wife's return was an event of considerable excitement. For these the women paid by knitting during the winter. Into the question of the dress of the present as compared with the past, it is scarcely my business to enter. For my own part I cannot see that any fault can be found with the tweed suits worn by our young men, though their fathers will affirm that there is nothing like the homespun. Then, too, the young girls are, as a rule, comely in their attire, though their mothers look back with regret upon the dark blue woollen stuffs of the maidens' own spinning, worn in their days. Dr. Milner Fothergill, in a paper he contributed to *Good Words,* on the subject of dress, a few months ago, contended, and I think rightly, for *warmth* and *suitability,* two features that should ever be borne in mind. Owing to the introduction of machinery, knitting has fallen into disuse, and notwithstanding other advantages you are, from a pecuniary point of view, losers by the change. In those days more money was cleared and saved. Indeed, in the dale of Dent, I understand that farms have been purchased by this branch of industry, and so essential was it as an aid to subsistence, that early in the century, when the revolutionizing influence of machinery began to be felt, some of the inhabitants of your Dale were forced to leave and migrate to the manufacturing towns, especially Bradford.

The dalesmen of the latter end of the last century and the beginning of this, were not without their amusements. Their favourite recreation was, I understand, fox hunting. They dearly loved a chase. I am indebted to Mr. Metcalfe-Gibson for the following: One Sunday morning whilst Divine Service was being held, the old parish clerk became aware that a fox hunt was going on, the dogs being at full cry. Being himself a keen fox hunter, he was more interested in the hunt than in the service. The dogs lost scent; this was perceived by John Fothergill, the parish clerk. Now they are on his track. The clerk excited by the fact said, instead of what he should have said in the Church Service, "Ah, they have him again." On another occasion Master Reynard was run to earth. Some of the men dug down until they came to a crevice in the rock, into which the fox had crept, when "Fox Willie," a well-known character, put his arm in to seize the fox. The men then called out, "Has ta got haud." "We've baith got haud, – pull away." Whereupon he was drawn out by his feet, fox and all.

I have said that they did their knitting exclusively by firelight; but at some other times they used rushlights. Indeed, this was the only light they used, when they used one at all. The rushes were cut and gathered on the fell, and hung up in bundles upon crooks in the kitchen ceiling. For use they were peeled almost, but not quite all round, and then dipped in the fat of sheep or rough grease of the house that was saved up for that purpose. "When the rush was ready it was placed in a candlestick which somewhat resembled nippers, and as it burnt on, was pushed through. The light shed was at the best but feeble, and so did little more than make the darkness visible. And yet people in well-to-do circumstances used the light almost exclusively.

Mr. Geo. Blades informed me as an example, that the grandfather and grandmother of Mr. William Cleasby, who lived at Aisgill, did not burn more than one pound of "white candles" in the year. I have been told the following anecdote of a man who had come from some other parish, and saw for the first time a pair of snuffers. He picked them up, looked at them, saw in part their design, and then, snuffing the candle with his finger and thumb, deposited the burnt wick in the box of the snuffers. Then, looking up with the air of a discoverer, remarked, "Very ingenious things!"

As in the adjoining parish of Ravenstonedale, sales were called in the church yard on Sunday morning, after divine service. Once a year there was "Shoemakers' Sunday," on which day the people assembled at "The King's Head," and paid their shoemakers' bills. The Sunday fell in August on St. Crispin's day, the shoemakers' patron saint, and just before the fair at Settle, at which the shoemakers bought their leather. The day was characterised by drinking, and an amount of holiday dissipation. There was one well known character – "Joss Dick" – who used to spend a great deal of his time, at the season, in cutting down rushes, which he sold down the country, as well as stones for stoning. Moss besoms, too, were generally used here; and the particular kind of moss being abundant in the dale, they were exported. They also made besoms of birch twigs, and their creels also they made themselves. Of these things not a single specimen remains. A few decrepit spinning-wheels are among you, which tell a tale of bygone days, when the dale was more self-contained than it is now, and the people realised themselves more fully to be a community of themselves, rather than as a fringe of a great population. Your gills were haunted, and the impending shadows of the almost perpendicular ridge on either side gave an austerity – I had almost said a foreboding superstition – to your fathers. "There was the steamlike spray which rose from the waterfall on the mountain side in rainy weather, and which popular imagination transformed into an auld wife's kettle; there was, too, Rob Roy, who was said to inhabit a cave at Castlethwaite; and the black hen, which invariably frustrated all attempts to unearth the buried treasure – a chest of gold of Pendragon Castle, by scratching in at night the soil which had been dug out by day." Beautiful white ladies, it is said, had been seen walking about the ruins of Pendragon Castle at the witching hour of twelve o'clock at night. Also it was said a headless ghost had been seen coming out of the gate before the castle. And as an indication that the castle was regarded as the rendezvous of ghosts, I learn that two or three of the fields adjoining it are called "Boggles." Nor need we be surprised at this superstition. The desolate ruin, with broken windows and doorways, half seen and half hidden by bushes, would be likely to suggest supernatural visitants to the imaginative and credulous mind. In the *History of Ravenstonedale,* I had occasion to notice the charms the people used, as late as half-a-century ago, to ward off evil spirits. Miss Fawcett tells me that in your dale, fifty years ago, when the hearthstone of Deep Gill farm house was taken up, the discovery was made of two or three brown earthenware bottles, each bottle being full of crooked pins, which the residents used as a charm to keep off evil spirits.

I have also had communicated to me many what I may call fireside stories, that have been handed down through families, and of which I give a specimen. Two hundred years ago a man named Iveson, who had "an evil eye" and "an unlucky hand," went with his son to get wood. Now this Iveson was a man of hasty temper, and it appears that on this occasion he returned home with his son dead. His wife immediately charged him with having killed the boy, but he said that he had been killed by a clog of wood falling on him as they were loading the cart. Still his wife persisted "Thou's killed him." At that time the law of the land was in an unsettled state, and the matter was not enquired into. Still the man's conscience accused him, and he was heard at times impulsively to cry out, so that he received the nickname "Cry." His wife, too, ever after shouted after him, "Thou's killed my boy." Such stories furnish us with glimpses of the rude habits of the people. They were not civilized, as we recognize the meaning of that word; they were in the main, however, honest and truthful, and vigorous. They were self-reliant, and shrewd in their business relations, with a sharp eye to the main chance. Beneficial changes, however, have come here; for instead of never having a post, or of having it (which was the next step) twice in the week,* yon can receive and send away letters every day. Your houses are lit with paraffin lamps. You see the daily papers, and you hear the rattle almost all day long of the railway car and locomotive as they run on a lofty elevation through your dale. The mediaeval darkness has gone, indeed its lingering mist has retired, and you are now participating in many of the comforts and blessings of the nineteenth century.

From early days the children were taught in the Episcopal Chapel by the curate. Mr. Garthwaite was an exception; he was an excellent schoolmaster. And to his painstaking care in getting up and copying local information I am indebted for much of the material in these lectures. And permit me to say to you, the men

---

* Mr. John Dickenson and the late Rev. R. Robinson got up a petition twenty-four years ago, and it resulted in a delivery on Wednesdays and Fridays.

and women of to-day, that you will confer a benefit on posterity by writing down the facts of your own life, and of dale life generally. We are all apt to forget that to-day will soon belong to history, and a history which is ever becoming more remote and more involved in darkness, and you can furnish what will be specks of light, and the historical fire-fly, if I may so express myself, is not to be despised.

It was the custom of the boys here, as well as in most of the other parishes in the district, to bar out the school master. The elder ones took possession of the school-room, and bolted and barred themselves in, the duty of the younger ones being to supply the "garrison" with refreshments, such as gingerbread, apples, toffee, &c. The master, not without an inkling probably of what he might expect, appeared at the door at the usual time, and finding it fastened rapped loudly for admittance with the words, "You boys, let me in," uttered in a real or assumed irascible tone. But no; the bravest of the garrison appear at the window, and a parley is held. Then the written terms are handed out, and I am fortunate in possessing two specimens. The first is dated 1740, and is as follows:

	The comments of the master.
"Good morrow, master! we do understand That barring out hath been on every hand;	"The more fault."
Therefore no custom new we mean to raise, For it has been from ancient days.	"Prove that."
This day to play we think it is our due, And hope it may not be offence to you,	"This I can allow."
A month at Xmas we now require, A week at Shrovetide and at Easter we desire,	"By what law I do not know."

The same at Whitsunday it is our right,
And one thing more to yon we have to write,
All holy days (three in the year to be our rule)
To attend the chapel, but not appear at school.

The rod and ferula we shall lay by,
In hopes that yon will not our points untie;
And if our tasks should prove too hard to use, } "I may see."
You will our tender years excuse.

On what we have writ we think it fit to stand, } "And which
But ever must obey your just command: } stand?"
Pray grant us these, and then we will not fail } "A mighty monster
To treat you with a glass of Mallerstang ale. } to prevail."

To the order of this paper I subscribe my hand.
While you obey (as you say) every just command.
Signed

THOMAS GASCOIGNE.
Nov. 18, 1740.

The other barring out poetic piece I have, is dated September 27th, 1794, just in time to secure the holiday at Brough Hill, to which allusion is here made. It is longer and more learned in allusion than the preceding. Its first line is the same as that of the piece which I have given in my History and Traditions of Ravenstonedale, composed by the Ravenstonedale boys for their barring out; in other respects it is different. It is as follows:

MALLERSTANG FOREST

Rules between the master of Mallerstang School and the scholars at the barring out. Sept. 27th, 1794. Honoured Master,

> Be not surprised these lines should come to hand,
> The naked truth they'll let you understand:
> We aid our jovial crew do all disdain
> These ponderous fetters, and this cramping chain.
>
> As on our beds we all profoundly slept
> Into our chambers great Minerva crept,
> With awful looks there did great Pallas stand,
> Her dreadful Aegis* in her potent hand.
>
> And briefly thus: "Boys will you labour still?
> That you have play it is my sacred will;
> Therefore when you return again to school
> Despise your master's awful sovereign rule.
>
> Long hath he kept the helm, but now,
> Take *you* the helm and let *him* take the prow."
> Therefore when we returned to school again
> Your birchen sceptre we did quite disdain.
>
> Then lock'd the door when you did turn your back
> Then we did straight no recreation lack.
> This, and tomorrow, sir, we'll have for play,
> Also each feast and every holy day.
>
> Two days at Brough Hill we hope you'll remember
> That's the first of October and the last of September
> For every new scholar a day we desire,
> It being the old custom we do it require.

Thursday afternoon we likewise do crave,
And Saturday afternoon we're determined to have;
Twenty eight days at Christmas we have its true;
And seven at shrove-tide we claim as our due.

Also take care that you do punish none
Until Epiphany be pass'd and gone.
Sir, these demands are civil, pray consent
To sign this bill and grant us merriment.

For recompence whereof we will not fail
To give you and your friends a glass of ale.
From what is written we'll not yield one jot,
Its like the Persian law that alters not.

In witness whereof we the said parties have hereunto set our hands the day and year first above written.

HUGH BLENKHORN } Scholars
JAMES TENNANT   JOHN GARTHWAITE, Master
Witness
MILES HUTCHINSON   EDWD. COATES
ADAM ROBINSON   Bondsman

After this usual and well-understood rebellion on the part of the boys, the school duties were resumed, the master regarding it simply as one of the incidents of the year. And things went on much as they did before, except that the Rev. Mr. Fawcett, his daughters laughingly informed me, usually gave the scholars a tea

---

* A potent shield that was supposed to turn every one who looked upon into stone.

on the afternoon of the barring-out day! Mr. Garthwaite was succeeded by the Revs. J. Monkhouse, James Hunter, and John Fawcett, who were followed by Mr. Alderson, Mr. Robt. Fothergill, and others, until the passing of the Education Act, which introduced a new system.

One thing was obvious – that a new schoolroom was needed. The bishop had found fault, too, that the churchyard should be used as a playground. Several attempts were made to raise money to build a new schoolroom, but they failed. The names of the Revs. J. Fawcett, J. Brunskill, and Lancelot Jefferson, of Brough, must especially be mentioned in this connection.

Then came, owing to the Education Act, an order to build the school according to Government requirement. As the landlords could not agree on the mode of operation, a School Board was formed. The first members were Messrs. G. Blades, J. Steel, Matthew Metcalfe, George Dent, and Philip Harrison. They met for the first time after the election, April 1, 1876. Mr. G. Blades was elected chairman. The members determined upon plans and specifications for a new board school, to be submitted to the lords of the Education Department. The architect was Mr. Smith – John Parker, of Stricklandgate, the mason; Thomas Fothergill, Nateby, slater; Wm. Jackson, Kirkby Stephen, joiner and painter; Robert Armstrong, plasterer; – Thornton, plumber. Cost, £529. Side by side with this it may interest you to know what your fathers thought of the cost of building a suitable schoolroom. Through the kindness of Miss Fawcett, I have an estimate, drawn up and submitted to a meeting holden at Mallerstang Chapel, the 4th day of October, 1826. It is as follows:

An Estimate For Building A Schoolhouse In Mallerstang.

	£	s.	d.
To Cutting Ground Works.	0	9	0
To Quarrying Stones for 112 Yards of Wall	1	17	4
To Leading 111 yards of Stones, at 4d. per yard	1	17	4
To Walling 112 yards of Wall, at ls. per yard	5	12	0
To Corner Stones and Lintels	2	2	6
To Flaggs and Flagging	6	3	0
To Slate and Slating	9	2	0
To Lime, Mixing Lime, and Plastering	4	7	0
To Work, Workmanship, Timbering, Seating	31	15	0
To Glazing Windows	3	12	0
To Grate, Door, Hinges, Nails, &c	2	11	0
	£69	12	2
At a meeting holden at Mallerstang Chapel, on Wednesday, the 4 day of Oct., 1826, it was computed the inhabitants of Mallerstang would subscribe the sum of	10	0	0
	£59	12	2

Rev. JOHN FAWCETT, Assistant Curate.
JOHN FOTHERGILL, Chapel Warden.
RICHAHD TUNSTALL.
ROBERT HUTCHINSON.
JOHN GARTHWAITE.
GEORGE BLADES.
EDWARD CLEASBY.

There is some contrast between £529 and £69 12s. 2d. But you must bear in mind that the price both of material and labour have greatly increased since then. In 1826 the locomotive steam-engine was in its infancy, and no one ventured to dream of the revolution it would accomplish in society. In 1876 that revolution had come, and the result to you was that your school building was more costly. Of course the estimated building of fifty years before would have been much simpler in its character, much of the work would have been not only at a lower rate than it was six years ago; it would have been cheerfully given, and the homely economy which I have observed in many departments of dale life would have been exercised. However, the building in which we are now assembled is in the course of being paid for, I understand, and is a credit to the valley. The school was opened on September 11th, 1877. The children had a free tea, given them on the occasion. Miss Gordon was appointed mistress. The present mistress is Miss Mary Jane Lawson. The following may interest you: "The Register of Mortgage of the Mallerstang School Board pursuant to 10th Victoria, chap. xvi, sec. 75-76. Date of deed, August 4th, 1877. Amount of mortgage, £529. Mallerstang School Board of the one part, and Williamson Willink, Esq., Secretary to the Public Works Loan Commissioners, of the other part, to be repaid in 50 years, £22 11s. to be paid on the 4th of August, 1878, and on every succeeding year up to and including the 4th day of August, 1926. The deed was registered August 6th, 1877."

The Wesleyan Chapel was opened on the first Sunday in June, 1879, by the Rev. Mr. Despres. It was erected chiefly through the exertions of Mr. G. Dent, the late Mr. Joseph King, and others. A Sunday-school is taught in connection with the chapel. The foundation stone was laid by Mr. Pighills, Mr. A. Dent, Miss Dent, and Miss Thompson. A "class" had been held here some time before 1879, and the building of the chapel was a necessity to accommodate the members of the Methodist Society here. And though I am no advocate for the multiplication of little places of worship in a stationary or a diminishing population, of course each section of the Church has a right to look after its own.

The following chronicle of the weather, and various incidents, has been handed to me by Captain Grimshaw, and it will, I have no doubt, be interesting to you. It was copied from an old book

> "The drouty somer was in ye year 1737.
> The following year was a very fortherly spring.
> It was on Sunday ye 25th day of February 1738-9 }
> That we had 2 hifes of Beas yt did bear Loadings. }
> On the 15th of June 1745 I was on hesengill woad
> And I see in a quoave [cove] hole a drift of snow."

On the 15th day of June 1749 being Thursday, Wildbore fell was covered with snow, & likewise Outhgill edge. And that night was exceeding hard frost so hard as there was water in dubs frose over.

—

In the year 1763 winter was pertuly [particularly?] wet with plases. The most flouds [floods] ever known and ye greatest damage in many.

—

In the year 1765 was the great droughty summer. It continued from about 5th of May to 31st August. Some few showers now & then. Most of ye springs dried up. Castle well we laded, it could not run down the gutter, nor betimes out of the well, it stood below the first step, it is flagged in the bottom, we watered a cow at Eden out of it.

—

1765. In August Butter Firkins was £1 6s. (?) Oatmeal 3s. per peck. Wheat 14s. 4d. per boul. A very little crop of hay got, we moed it one day and got it the next it was so very hot.

—

1776. The greatest sight of blossom ever seen and greatest quantity of fruit of all sorts boath orchards and woods that ever was known, and finest crops of corn that ever was seen. Apples in ye south contracted for ls. per bushell for 17000 bushell.

In the year 1778 & 9 scarce any snow or frost quite open all winter never the like seen. Everything in February as forward as some years in May.

—

2nd May 1772, A stormy spring hay 6d. per stone and all eat out. Hard frost every night this was 2nd May large snow drifts all along Outhgill Edge. I fed 2 hives of bees with honey in May 14th day, it was so stormy. Oat meal 2s. 6d. per peck. Oats 19s. p. load. Potatoes 10d. p. peck. Beef 4¼d. per pound. Veal 2¾d. p. pound. Good mutton 4d. per pound. Butter 10s. per stone, Wheat 15s. 8d. per bowel. It continued stormy and dry 10th, and frost every night till the 17th of May. Then was some warm rain & so continued well. 1767. 11th & 12 March. Jos: Fothergill of Southwaite in Mallerstang had a hive of bees cast boath day and knit, but went to the old hive again.

—

So ends an interesting chronicle, such as any of you might keep to-day.

The constituted authority of the dale is very much the same as that of the adjoining dales. There are two overseers; their names at the present time are Mr. William Bousfield and Mr. Richard Mason. There are two surveyors of the highways, Mr. William Metcalfe and Mr. John Bellas. There is one poor-law guardian who represents you on the poor-law board, elected annually. The guardian for this year is Mr. James Slinger of Cranberry. Your present poor rate value of the township is £3,340. The basis of county valuation fixed in quarter session in April, 1879, was £3,750. The game and fish, Captain Grimshaw informs me, belong to the customary holders. I understand that although you contribute a handsome sum, varying according to the difference of rate, to the maintenance of the poor, you have not received any parish relief, up to very recently, for the last thirty years. Fortunate indeed have been your circumstances, that there has not been one amongst you so poor as to need outside help. One of my first questions, on enquiring into the social condition of the dale, was, "Has the dale no charities? No good man whose memory it can bless, the effect of whose thoughtful munificence some of you are benefiting by to-day?" It has. In the year 1784, on the 8th of May, Geo. Middleton, of Sedbergh, bequeathed £100, the interest of which should be applied to the giving of bread to the poor in the Church every Sabbath morning. The money was well laid out, and now yields, on an average, £30 per annum. Lancelot Hunter, who died in 1731, left £10 to the poor of the dale of Mallerstang. This money, too, was laid out in cattle gates, and now yields, on an average, £5 per annum. This money is given away on Christmas Day to the poor.

These names are not known probably beyond the limits of your dale. Though dead, they still speak. They speak words of practical comfort. to one section of you, and to another of sacred emulation. And though you do not know what poverty is in its deepest sense, a recipient of parish relief being a rare person – as he ever has been – in your midst, you are not, nevertheless, the inhabitants of so happy a valley as to be without those to whom the legacies of prosperous men of the past are not a source of comfort and of help.* Self-contained, in the sense in which your fathers were, you are not – nor can you be, nor would it be good for you – but in provision for the poor and less fortunate, the more self-contained you are the better.

The Midland railway extension from Settle to Carlisle was opened for passenger traffic on the lst of May, 1876. That portion

---

* See Appendix, page 123.

of it which passes through your dale commences south at Aisgill Moor, and ends at Birket tunnel, and during the whole distance there is no station for the accommodation of the inhabitants; this has been found to be a considerable inconvenience, inasmuch as in the old days the traffic on the highway between Hawes and Kirkby Stephen was very considerable, and the necessaries of life were brought by carriers and dealers almost to the threshold of the farmer; but since the construction of the line the inhabitants have been deprived of that accommodation, carriers being no longer necessary.* At the present time, however, there is, as you know, considerable agitation going on in your midst, for the erection of a station in your dale, which those of us who are outside, and you especially who are inside, see to be necessary. At the head of Mallerstang, which is its highest point, the line is at an elevation of 1167 feet above the sea, and in its entire length it is at a considerable elevation from the dale. During its construction there was quite an invasion of the navvy class, who mostly lived in huts at Birket and Aisgill. I understand that their mural influence here was not good, to say the least of it. By this time I trust that every trace of its baleful effect has gone. For some time after the passenger trains had commenced running they attracted the attention of the people of the dale, and I have been informed that during the haytime of that year, the haymakers were continually arrested in their work by watching them. Then at night they attracted as much attention as they did by day, and seemed more wonderful, lit up and rushing on, against the sombre background of Wild Boar Fell. Now, I suppose, you scarcely see them. Meanwhile they are an important element of education

---

* See Appendix, page 123.

here. They make you realise that there is an England beyond what you see of it. They suggest travel to you, and furnish you with facilities for carrying out your wish They weaken in adult life the rooted feeling that your fathers had for the place. The patriotism for the dale is not less, but the local prejudice is. In olden times a man who went from Shorgill to Outhgill to live, a distance under 300 yards, though another division merely of his own dale, asked his clergyman what he had done to be transported? In those days many of the inhabitants were born, brought up, lived to old age, and died in the dale, without going beyond it. Their world was Mallerstang. Their king was Lord de Clifford or Lord Thanet. Their primate was the incumbent of the Mother Church, at Kirkby Stephen, under whom, in those days, their own minister laboured as a curate, and their great sensation of the year was Brough Hill Fair.

Some look back with wistful regret upon "the good old times"; with such I have no sympathy. But I do say, that for the race of yeomen, or statesmen, as you call them, who are passing away, I entertain a profound respect, and of whom only two remain in the dale – Mr. Thomas Blades and Mr. Philip Harrison – and I believe the time has very nearly, if not quite, come when something should be done – I do not know what; I have no political nostrum on the subject when this class of men shall be reinstated; and that we may again see the land, not in the hands of the few, and that increasingly as at present, but the many sturdy, self respecting, well-informed and independent men, such as many of your fore-elders were; who in the time of commotion or change in this country, should it come, would be on the side of order, as a tower of strength.

—

The readers who have proceeded with me so far, will, I am quite sure, thank me for concluding this Lecture with a paper by the Rev. W. Thompson, M.A., of Sedbergh. He is the curate there, and is withal a scholarly man. He says -

"I have put together a few reminiscences of Mallerstang life as I knew it some thirty years ago. Short as is the retrospcet, it reaches back to the days before the steam engine had puffed away many an old-world notion and custom from among us. We had then but little intercourse with the great world outside us, and might be regarded as the unadulterated produce of the dale, and the genuine inheritors of the dialect and traditions of the past. We were, in fact, eleven miles or so from the nearest railway station, and many of the older generation lived and died without ever having seen a locomotive. A weekly newspaper or two found their way into the dale, and were handed about until the next number made its appearance and entered on a similar circuit. Our occupations were of a truly rural nature, the usual routine of a small grazing farm being varied only by clippings and sheep-washings, haymaking, mowing 'bedding,' or cutting peats and 'flawes.' We were a clannish folk, and not fond of strangers. But there were three times in the year when we might expect to see them in unusual numbers, and these were always seasons of great excitement to the rising generation. The first was Outhgill Fair, now numbered among the bygones; the second was when the droves of sheep and cattle from Scotland were on their way to the Yorkshire fairs; and the third was about the time of Brough Hill Fair, when for several days a miscellaneous panorama of men and things defiled through the dale. Some of the more notable characters were eagerly looked for every year, and their reappearance was hailed with delight. Such was the case in particular with that unfailing Brough Hill-er, the man who had forsworn the use of a hat.

"The only resident gentlemen we had among us were the parson and the schoolmaster. The postman and the policeman had not yet found us out. If any one thought it necessary to write to us, his letter would be helped on somehow, generally by some obliging farmer, on the market-day. A native constable, periodically chosen by the ratepayers, sufficed to keep us in order. He was entrusted with the custody of a truncheon, as the emblem and possible instrument of his office. It bore a strong resemblance to a blue rolling-pin, tapered at one end to form a handle, and emblazoned at the other with a gilt lion and unicorn. It was occasionally produced for admiring inspection at children's parties, but seldom required to be wielded on the field of battle, for we were a peaceable people, as a rule, the exception being when that bone of contention – the best share of the fell-set us by the ears, and then we felt that we might justifiably indulge in a few rounds at fisticuffs.

"'Haverbread' and 'blue-milk' cheese were our standing dishes, fustian and clogs our working-clay attire, rushlights and farthing candles our illumination, and we had a rich and expressive vernacular, not understanded of the Southron; but we managed to live an honest and happy, if somewhat homely life. If any one was ill, the doctor was a long way off, so we put faith in 'yerbs,' and awaited the result with patience; while in cases of urgency the ladies were looked after by an experienced matron without a diploma. We seemed reluctant to grow old, and I remember that 'the Sycamore lads,'* as they continued to be called to the last, were fine specimens of youthfulness at sixty years of age and upwards. It was necessary, however, that we

---

*Three stalwart bachelor brothers who lived at the farm called 'Sycamores.'

should die sometimes, and then the whole dale was 'warned' to the funeral, and representatives from nearly every house showed that we took a mutual interest in each others' joys and sorrows.

"Among recollections of boyish interest I may note the capture of 'bullyfrogs' and 'tommyloaches' in Outhgill Beck, and the tickling of trout in the river Eden. Then, at the proper season, there were strawberries in Shortgill Wood, and curiously-streaked snail shells among them withal. Blackberries and cranberries sometimes allured us to the higher grounds, but 'bumblykites' and 'brown-leamers' were to be had nearer to hand; and even 'choups' and 'heckberries' were not always despised. Sometimes we were seized with ambition for remoter scenes, when a voyage of exploration would be made to the old coal-pit on one side of the valley, or to the top of Wild Boar on the other.

"The Fifth of November was a day much to be observed among us, and we visited every house in due order with a view to obtaining cash for the purchase of tar-barrels and other combustibles. We invariably announced our presence by the blowing of horns and the reciting of a time-honoured ditty, setting forth the obligation of a proper recognition of Gunpowder Plot. It was rarely that we failed in extracting the needful coin; but if such a calamity should ensue, we were equally prepared with another poetical effusion, which boded much evil to the members of that unhappy household. Nor were we, on less public occasions, without our indoor enjoyments, when the long winter evenings set in. Our elders were at all times fond of 'going a-sitting' to each others houses, and too often indulged in ghost-stories and tales of the uncanny and the marvellous. I could view with equanimity the steam-like spray rising from a waterfall on the mountain side in rainy weather, which popular imagination transformed into an 'auld wife's kettle,' but I had a real dread of Rob Roy, who was said to inhabit a cave at Castlethwaite, and of the old black hen, which invariably frustrated all attempts to unearth the buried treasure at Pendragon Castle, by scratching in at night the soil which had been dug out by day. 'Toffee-joins' were rare fun to the youngsters, while at 'merry-neets' the lads and lasses of a larger growth tripped it blithely to the accompaniment of fiddle, concertina, or dulcimer, for pianos were quite unknown. But of all delights perhaps none fluttered the juvenile breast more than the announcement that a monster circus or menagerie was about to visit Kirkby Stephen; and though it was five miles thither and five miles back, the pranks of the clown and the uncouth ways of the wild beasts had charms which few 'Mauston' lads could resist; and we lightened the journey with a look at the leech-pond at Dale-foot, and with equestrian performances on the donkeys which frequented the roadside near Wharton Park.

"I have one more reminiscence, and that is connected with the school and the church. After entering the porch of the latter, a well-worn flight of stone steps led to an upper room, in which the children of the dale were taught reading, writing, and a modicum of arithmetic. This room always bulked large in my imagination, until I lately visited it again, when it seemed wonderfully dwarfed in its dimensions, and I found it no longer the centre of learning, a brand-new Board School having completely eclipsed its glory. The church, too, was not the church of my childhood. The old longitudinal oak pews had given place to cross-benches of a modern pattern, and the towering three-decker had dwindled to a mere shadow of its former self. Even the loaves of Middleton's Charity, which used to be displayed on one of the window-ledges, had secured more eligible quarters in a gilded case. A new vestry had broken out; and I pictured to myself, by way of contrast, the dingy surplice which used to be laid over the back of one of the pews, waiting to be donned in the body of the church. I seemed to hear again the sonorous voice of old James Middleton giving out a Psalm from Tate and Brady, and pitching the note with a preliminary tootle on the flute, while the clergyman took that and other opportunities of recruiting his energies with a pinch of snuff: I mused on all this, and much besides. I could not conscientiously say 'the old was better,' but I indulged a momentary pang of regret that so many of the visible mementos of my own happy Mallerstang childhood were for ever vanishing away."

NOTE. – To readers unacquainted with the dialect the following brief explanations may be welcome:"Bedding," rushes for cattle to lie on. "Flawes," turf for fuel, otherwise styled "flouts," or "turves." "Haverbread," oatcake. "Blue-milk," skimmed milk. "Yerbs," herbs. "Warned," invited. "Bully-frogs," bullheads or millers' thumbs. "Tommy-loaches," loaches. "Bumblykites," black-berries or bramble-berries. To a Mallerstangian the term "blackberries" would suggest blackcurrants. "Brown-leamers," hazel-nuts ripe and ready to leave the husks. "Choups" the heps of the wild rose. "Heck-berries," the fruit of the bird-cherry. "Going a-sitting," visiting each others' houses in the evening for company and conversation. "Toffee-joins," entertainments at which a number of young persons resolved themselves into a joint stock company limited, for the production and distribution of a panful of toffee. "Mauston," the native pronounciation of Mallerstang.

APPENDIX.

NOTE A, PAGE 37.

POSSIBLY it has become obvious to the reader of archaeological sympathies that Mallerstang is particularly rich in ancient words. For the meanings of many of the following words I am indebted to Canon Simpson. Amongst the names of the different divisions of the dale there is *Anger-holme*, pronounced Angram, which means fertile meadow. *Ais Gill*, water gill. The word "gill" is Icelandic (gil) for ravine. *Hanging Lund*, a wood on the side of a hill. The word "lund" means shelter, and especially from wind. *Southwaite*, south clearing. *Castlethwaite*, the castle clearing. *Hazel Gill*, the "gill" overshaded by hazel bushes. There are a few hazel bushes still there. *Elm Gill*; the "gill" derived its name evidently from an elm tree, or elms that distinguished it. There are elm trees about this gill still. *Far Cote Gill*; the word "cote" was applied to any building or shelter, hence "far cote" is in distinction from some other. There is also "nar," (near) cote gill. The word peat cote, as applied to a building to put peat in, is still used on the other side the county. *Cote Gill Grains*; the word grains means spread out. *Sand Pot*, name possibly derived from the river opposite it throwing up large banks of sand; hence a place from which sand could be obtained. *Cove*, a hollow place. The same word is applied to a small harbour, a part of the shore hollowed out by water. There are many coves in Mallerstang, and they are distinguished by some characteristic term, such as "Dove Coves," "Pike Coves," "Turn-at Coves," "Rowantree Coves." There is a beck called "Old Hush." The word "hush" is used in the dialect still, a descriptive of a rush of water. There are two chalybeate springs in the dale. They are situated not far from each other, and on the eastern side. The one is High Rigg Well, and the other is near Joseph's Gill. *Dragon's Den,* a spot on Wildboar Fell which the dragon was supposed to frequent, and which it is thought by some gives its name to Pendragon Castle. A fabulous monster that preyed upon men, women, and innocent children, and concealed itself in its den whilst taking its repose. *Great Bell,* situated at Dale Foot, 1,230 feet high. There are several "bells" in the county – e.g., Green Bell in Ravenstonedale. Some suppose that the name is taken from the form, and others that it is a Celtic word and a corruption of Baal, Baal having been worshipped by the Druids on high hills. In the boundary ridings we meet continually with the expression, "As Heaven's water deals" – a primitive and poetic expression for water shed.

Some of my readers may be interested to know that the turnpike road at the division of Yorkshire and Westmorland is 1194·8 feet above the sea level, according to the Ordnance map.

NOTE B, PAGE 59.

I have been furnished with "a list of persons who have held the office of lords bailiff for the township of Mallerstang for the last ninety years, commencing with the year 1793:

James Atkinson, Dale Foot, 44 years.

Robert Atkinson, Dale Foot, 22 years.

Parkin Blades, Outhgill, 16 years.

Thomas Blades, Outhgill, the present bailiff, who has been in that position for the last eight years."

NOTE C, PAGE 113.

There is an almshouse at Appleby for widows, founded by Lady Anne, Countess of Pembroke. Amongst Mr. Garthwaite's MSS. I find the following petition from Alice Collin, of Mallerstang, had been presented to the Earl of Thanet:

"*To the Right Honourable Sacville, Earl of Thanet. The humble petition of Alice Collin, widow, most humbly sheweth -*

"Your petitioner, who is in the 62nd year of her age, is the relict of John Collin, of Mallerstang, in the county of Westmorland, and her father, Henry Robinson, was a tenant under your lordship in the dale of Mallerstang aforesaid.

"Your petitioner's husband held a small farm of your lordship, and with unfeigned gratitude your petitioner acknowledges your lordship's goodness having been extended towards her in the continuance of the said farm.

"Your lordship's petitioner, suffering under afflictions and corporeal infirmities, hastened by age, labouring under a weak frame of body (ill-supported by a tender constitution), has humbly made bold to implore your lordship's benevolent kindness to admit your petitioner into the Hospital at Appleby when a vacancy may occur, and it may seem meet to your lordship. This, which should your petitioner be so happy as to obtain, it will, with the utmost humility, be ever gratefully acknowledged. And your petitioner (as in duty bound) will ever pray, &c.

"We, the undersigned, do certify to the truth of the above, and do humbly recommend the petitioner to your lordship's notice and protection,

"Witness our hands this 19th day of September, 1809.

"JOHN GARTHWAITE

"CHRISTOPHER ROBINSON."

The petitioner died before a vacancy occurred.

NOTE D, PAGE 114.

The inhabitants finding the inconvenience of not having a railway station, application was made to the Midland Company, through Mr. W. Lowther, M.P., one of the members for the county, who made a representation to the Directors of the aforesaid company. Accordingly an inspector was sent down, who, after making a careful examination of the line and probable traffic, &c., reported. As a result of this the manager, Mr. Noble, stated that a station would necessitate the construction of a road of approach, 500 yards long, and a bridge, and that the outlay would not pay. Consequently the dale folks must wait a little longer. Subsequently an influential meeting of the landholders, presided over by the Rev. W. Alnwick, was held in the Board School, to take into consideration the question whether they were prepared to construct the road provided that the railway company would erect a station. The majority were of opinion that the landholders would be willing to construct a road. Meanwhile the matter was referred to a committee appointed at that meeting.

There is considerable sympathy with the folks of Mallerstang in this matter, which has expressed itself in a series of interesting and earnest letters, which have appeared in the newspapers, from those living within and without the dale. We all hope that a railway station at Mallerstang will soon be an accomplished fact. To tourists such a station would be a great advantage. At present Mallerstang is reached from the south by leaving the train at Hawes Junction, and from the north by Kirkby Stephen, either on the Midland or London and North-Eastern Railway. The northern boundary of Mallerstang is 2½ miles from Kirkby Stephen.

In conclusion, I take this opportunity of thanking the many people of Mallerstang, whose names I have not mentioned, for their kindness in furnishing me with information, and in many ways shewing sympathy with me in this work. One marked feature of the folks of Mallerstang is warm-hearted hospitality, and I hope it may ever continue. It so happens that whilst concluding the MS. of this history I am preparing to leave this county for the neighbouring one of Lancashire. If I were a poet I would write a farewell poem, but as I am not I content myself with adopting, as my own, the words of Mr. Alfred Tennyson, and say, "True and tender north," farewell.

LIST OF SUBSCRIBERS

Lord Hothfield, 4 copies; Lord Bective, 12 copies.

Rev. J. Allatt, 1copy; Rev. R. Alliott, M.A., 2; J. 0. Atkinson, Esq., E. Armitage, Esq., 8; Mr. 0. Allen, Rev. W. Alnwick, Rev. G. W. Atkinson, T. A. Argles, Esq., Mrs. Allen, Mr. Geo. Alderson, Mr. James Airey, Mrs. Ann Atkinson, Mr. John Atkinson.

A. J. Burgess, Esq., 2 copies; J. K. Butcher, Esq., Mr. Jas. Bell, Rev. W. Burrows, B.A., Mrs. Beck, Rev. W. Bowman, Rev. J. Brown, B.A., Mr. Edw. Beck, Mr. Thos. Bousfield, Mr. J. W. Braithwaite, J. Brunskill, Esq., Colonel Burn, W. Lloyd Birbeck, Esq., 2; Amos Beardsley, Esq., R. H. Beardsley, Esq., Robert Blair, Esq., Mr. T. L. Buck, H. J. Blanc, Esq., G. F. Braithwaite, Esq., 3; J. B. Bailey, Esq., Mr. Butt, Mr. Jos. Brunskill, Mr. L. Burton, Mr. Jas. Bradbury, Mr. Wm. Bradbury, Mr. H. Beck, Thos. Blades, Esq., 6; Mr. M. Burnop, Mr. R. Blackett.

J Cropper, Esq., M.P., 2 copies; J. B. Cook, Esq., 2; J. Carver, Esq., 4; W. Carver, Esq., 4; Miss Carver, 2; Mrs. Chamberlain, 4; Captain J. W. Cameron, Rev. J. Chapelhow, Rev. S. Clarkson, Mrs. Copeland, J. F. Crosthwaite, Esq., T. Carrick, Esq., Rev. Thos. Calvert, Wm. Cleasby, Esq., 4; Mr. Jos. Clark, Mr. Thos. Cleasby, Mr. Marsh Clementson, Rev. J. Calvert.

Sir George Duckett, Bart., 1 copy; Mr. John Dickinson, 4; Thos.

Dover, Esq., Edw. Dover, Esq., Mr. Thos. Dixon, Miss Dixon, Causeway End, A. C. Dent, Esq., Mr. John Dent, Mr. Geo. Dent, 2; Mr. Aaron Davis, E. B. Dawson, Esq., J.P., Miss S. Dawson.

Dr. Edger, 1copy; Mr. Mark Ellwood.

J. M. Fothergill, Esq., M.D., 2 copies; W. Furness, Esq., 2; Robert Furness, Esq., Mr. A. Faulkener, J. R. Foster, Esq., Rev. E. Forster, Miss Fawcett, 5; H. Fell, Esq., Rev. E. H. Raven-Ermcote, R. S. Ferguson, Esq., F.A.S., 2; Mr. Robinson Fawcett, Mr. Wm. Fothergill, Mrs. Margt. Fothergill, 2.

Capt. Grimshaw, 8 copies; A. M. Gibson, Esq., 3; A. M. Gibson, Esq., jun., Atkinson M Gibson, Esq., Thos. Gibson, Esq., M.D., 2; Mr. Gray, Antiquarian and Topographical Bookseller, Manchester, 6; Rev. W. B. Grenside, M.A.

Hon. G. Howard, M.P., J. Harker, Esq., MD, 4 copies; Mr. Hogg, 4; Rev. J. Holroyd, Mr. w Harper, Mrs. J. Hewetson, Rev. A. Howson, Mr. W. Hutchinson, 2; Rev. J. Harrison, Miss Hunter, Mr. John Hutchinson, Mr. J. Hunter, Mr. P. Harrison, 3; Mr. Edw. Hutchinson, Mrs. H. Hewetson, H. Hewetson, Esq., Rev. J. Hall, Rev. J. Heap, Thos. Howson, Esq., Miss Hill, 2; F. Hall, Esq., Mrs. Hunter, Robert Hewetson, Esq., Miss Hodgson, Jas. Hudson, Esq., J. E. Hargreaves, Esq., J. C. Hetherington, Esq., J. Hutchinson, Esq., 6; Mr. R. Heygarth. J. G. Johnson, Esq., 8 copies; Rev. D. M. Jenkins, W. Jackson, Esq.,

F.S.A., H. J. Jenkinson, Esq. Rev. H. Kendall, Wm. Kilvington, Esq., Mr. Thos. Kirkbride, Mr. Jas. Knewstubb, Mrs. Jane King, Mr. Thos. King. Honble. W. Lowther, M.P., 1 copy; Rev. R. G. Leigh, 2; Rev. T. Lawson, Rev. J. Lees.

W. Milner, Esq., 6 copies; S. Massey. Esq., 6; Roderick Maclaren, Esq., 2; Thos. Mason, Esq., 2; Mr. Moorhouse, Rev. H. W. Mote, J. G. Mounsey, Esq., Mr. Thos. Metcalfe; Mr. S. Milner, Mr. Massey, H. Milner, Esq., J. S. Metcalfe, Esq., Mr. Chris. Metcalfe,

Mr. Robinson Moor, Mr. L. Mason, Mr. Wm. Metcalfe, Mr. R. Mason, Mr. Edw. Metcalfe, Rev. J. A. Macfadyan, D.D.

J. Nicholls, Esq., 2 copies; Mr. John Nicholson, Mr. J. W. Nicholson,

J. H. Nicholson, Esq., M.A., Richard Nelson, Esq.

Thos. H. Preston, Esq., 4 copies; Miss Powley, R. Preston, Esq., 2; Mr. R. Peacock, Rev. W. Pink, Mr. M. Pratt, Mr. W. Potter, Rev. R. V. Pryce, M.A.

H. Richardson, Esq., 1 copy; H. F. Rigge, Esq., John Robinson, Esq., John Robinson, Esq., F.G.S., F. J. Robinson, Esq., R. S. Robinson, Esq.,

J. H. Robinson, Esq., Mrs. Robinson, W. Robinson, Esq., Mr. R Rennison, Mr. Thos. Richardson, Mr. Adam Robinson.

Rev. Canon Simpson, 4 copies; Rev. J. Straffen, 2; Dr. Sayer, 2;

Mrs. Slade, 2; Mr. R. Shaw, 4; Rev. Thos. Slevan, J. S. Smith, Esq., Rev. J. H. Sumner, Rev. M. H. Sharp, Jos. Simpson, Esq., Mr. Miles Shepherd, Miss Shaw, Thos. Shaw, Esq.

Rev. W. Thompson, M.A., 10 copies; R. Thexton, Esq., 4; Mrs. Thompson, 2; Mr. J. Tanner, Mr. T. Tanner, Rev. W. Taylor, Mr. R. Thornborrow, Rev. Canon Troutbeck, Rev. H. Tarrant, J.R. Vaizey, Esq.

W. H. Wakefield, Esq., 12 copies; Ald. Whitehead, 5; Rev. J. E. Whitehead, Rev. T. Windsor, Mr. White, Mr. A. Wharton, Rev. B. Wilkinson, Rev. J. Wharton, Rev. H. Wallace, W. Wiper, Esq., 2; Rev. Canon Ware, Rev. G. F. Weston, 2; J. F. Wilson, Esq., Mr. R. Wilson, Mr. Jas. Winder, Mr. Jas. Wearing, Mr. Thos. Wade.

JOHN HEYWOOD, Excelsior Steam Printing and Bookbinding Works,
Hulme Hall Road, Manchester.